HOLT
2
GERMAN

Activities for Communication

HOLT, RINEHART AND WINSTON

A Harcourt Classroom Education Company

Austin · New York · Orlando · Atlanta · San Francisco · Boston · Dallas · Toronto · London

Contributing Writer

Cindy Reinke-Pressnall

Cover Photo/Illustration Credits
Group of students: George Winkler/HRW Photo; German sign: George Winkler/HRW Photo
CD: Digital imagery® © 2003 Photodisc, Inc.

KOMM MIT! is a trademark licensed to Holt, Rinehart and Winston, registered in the United States of America and/or other jurisdictions.

Printed in the United States of America

ISBN 0-03-065578-1

6 7 8 9 10 11 018 11 10 09 08 07

Contents

SITUATION CARDS

To the Teacher

Oral communication is the most challenging language skill to develop and test. The *Komm mit!* *Activities for Communication* book helps students to develop their speaking skills and gives them opportunities to communicate in many different situations. The Communicative Activities and Situation Cards provide a variety of information-gap activities, role-playing scenarios, and interviews to assist students with the progression from closed-ended practice to more creative, open-ended use of German. The Realia reproduces authentic documents to provide students with additional reading practice using material written by and for native speakers. Included with the Realia are teaching suggestions and student activities showing how to integrate the four skills and culture into your realia lesson. With the focus on dialogue and real-life context, the activities in this book will help your students achieve the goal of genuine interaction.

Each chapter of *Activities for Communication* provides:

- **Communicative Activities** In each chapter three communicative, pair-work activities encourage students to use German in realistic conversation, in settings where they must seek and share information. The activities provide cooperative language practice and encourage students to take risks with language in a relaxed, uninhibiting, and enjoyable setting. The activities correspond to each **Stufe** and encourage use of functions, vocabulary, and grammar presented in that chapter section. Each activity may be used upon completion of the **Stufe** as a Performance Assessment, or may be recorded on audio or video tape for inclusion in students' portfolios. The activities may also be used as an informal review of the **Stufe** to provide additional oral practice.

- **Realia** Each chapter contains three reproducible pieces of realia that relate to the chapter theme and reflect life and culture in the German-speaking countries. Finding they can read and understand documents intended for native speakers gives students a feeling of accomplishment that encourages them to continue learning. Upon completion of each **Stufe,** the realia may be used to review the functions, vocabulary, and grammar presented, or may be used as additional practice at any point within the **Stufe.** Along with the blackline masters of the realia you will find suggestions for using the realia in the classroom. These suggestions include a combination of activities for individual, pair, and group work and focus on the skills of listening, speaking, reading, and writing, while at the same time exploring authentic cultural information.

- **Situation Cards** For each **Stufe** of the twelve chapters, three sets of interview questions and three situations for role-playing are provided in blackline master form. These cards are designed to stimulate conversation and to prepare students for speaking tests. The interviews or role-playing may be used as pair work with the entire class, as activities to begin the class period, as oral performance assessments upon completion of the **Stufe,** or to encourage oral practice at any point during study of the **Stufe.** These conversations may be recorded as audio or video additions to students' portfolios. Because the cards may be recycled throughout the scholastic year as review of chapters already completed, students will be rewarded as they realize they are meeting goals and improving their communicative abilities. To avoid having to copy the cards repeatedly, consider mounting them on cardboard and laminating them. They may be filed for use during the year as well as for future classes.

Communicative Activities

Communicative Activity 1-1 A

a. You and your partner are master spies working in Vienna. Your boss, known to you only as 'Q', has told you that an enemy agent will be present at a dinner party being held this evening at the **Hofburg**. You and your partner obtain invitations and attend the party, where you assemble bits and pieces of information about the various guests in an effort to identify the spy. Now you and your partner have met in the basement to compile your knowledge and catch your opponent!

Quiz your partner in order to fill in the blanks in the table below. When you have both completed the chart, use the information at the bottom of the page to identify the spy.

Name	Aussehen	Eigenschaften	Interessen
Renate Geheimdienst	lange, blonde Haare; hübsch		fotografieren; Basketball
Katja Kugelförmig		unsportlich; intelligent	
Kaiser Schmarrn	schwarze Haare; trägt Kontaktlinsen		basteln; Briefmarken sammeln
Wilhelm Geck			Ski laufen; reisen
Gisela Gänsemarsch	vollschlank; grüne Augen	freundlich; tierlieb	
Anke Spitzel	schlank; kurze, hellbraune Haare		
Otto Wagner von Schnurrbart		sportlich; sympathisch	schwimmen; Fußball
Ulrike Unerträglich	rötliche Haare; blaue Augen		
Otto Vorbestraft		neugierig; nicht nett	tanzen; Golf
Helmut Taugenichts		lustig; unsportlich	

b. Using the data below, supplied by 'Q', find the spy.

The subject has either blond or red hair, perfect vision, and a charming, energetic personality. He or she doesn't know how to operate any technology more complicated than the wheel, and is tone deaf.

The name of the spy is: _____

Holt German 2 Komm mit!, Chapter 1   Activities for Communication   **1**

Communicative Activity 1-1 B

a. You and your partner are master spies working in Vienna. Your boss, known to you only as 'Q', has told you that an enemy agent will be present at a dinner party being held this evening at the **Hofburg**. You and your partner obtain invitations and attend the party, where you assemble bits and pieces of information about the various guests in an effort to identify the spy. Now you and your partner have met in the basement to compile your knowledge and catch your opponent!

Quiz your partner in order to fill in the blanks in the table below. When you have both completed the chart, use the information at the bottom of the page to identify the spy.

Name	Aussehen	Eigenschaften	Interessen
Renate Geheimdienst		kinderlieb; fleißig	
Katja Kugelförmig	rötliche Haare; nicht sehr attraktiv		Musik machen; ausgehen
Kaiser Schmarrn		unsympathisch; langweilig	
Wilhelm Geck	klein; lange, blonde Haare	faul; gut gelaunt	
Gisela Gänsemarsch			Tennis; zeichnen
Anke Spitzel		ruhig; nett	Rad fahren; kochen
Otto Wagner von Schnurrbart	hat eine Glatze; braune Augen		
Ulrike Unerträglich		schlecht gelaunt; nervös	lesen; malen
Otto Vorbestraft	graue Augen; attraktiv		
Helmut Taugenichts	groß; hat eine Brille		Comics sammeln; kochen

b. Using the data below, supplied by 'Q', find the spy.

The subject has either blond or red hair, perfect vision, and a charming, energetic personality. He or she doesn't know how to operate any technology more complicated than the wheel, and is tone deaf.

The name of the spy is: _____

Name _____ Klasse _____ Datum _____

a. You are looking at a catalog and placing an order by phone. Your partner is on the other end of the line taking down the information about your order. After you have placed your order, have your partner read it back to you to confirm that the information he or she has taken down is correct. Your partner will then tell you the total price (**Gesamtpreis**) that you owe.

Bestellschein

Kleidungsartikel	Katalognummer/ Seite	Größe	Farbe	Menge (*quantity*)	Preis
Bluse	108, S. 36	32	weiß	1	€22,50
Jeanshose	32, S. 42	M	blau	1	€25,00
Jeansjacke	56, S. 43	34	blau	1	€37,60
Shorts	110, S. 33	M	schwarz	2	€12,50
Rock	180, S. 10	38	dunkelblau	1	€34,00

b. This time you are the mail-order clerk, and you have in front of you the order that this customer placed last week. You think there were some errors when the order was transferred to the computer system, so you go through the order with the customer and correct anything that is incorrect. Tell the customer the total price (**Gesamtpreis**) of the order. Write your corrections in the blanks.

Bestellschein

Kleidungsartikel	Katalognummer/ Seite	Größe	Farbe	Menge (*quantity*)	Preis
Minirock	15, S. 72	34	schwarz	2	€17,50
Armband	106, S. 25	–	silber	3	€12,50 (x3)
Handtasche	125, S. 32	–	grau	1	€22,50
Schuhe	20, S. 15	L	braun	1 Paar	€10,00
Mütze	22, S. 28	M	rot, blau und weiß	2	€6,25 (x2)

Communicative Activity 1-2 B

a. You work for a mail-order company. It is your job to take orders that are called in and then to make sure that they are filled properly. Someone (your partner) has just called in with an order. Take the order, fill out the form (**Bestellschein**), and then repeat the order to the customer, telling him or her the total price (**Gesamtpreis**) of the order.

Bestellschein

Kleidungsartikel	Katalognummer/ Seite	Größe	Farbe	Menge (*quantity*)	Preis

b. You placed an order by phone last week, but somehow it got messed up in the company's computer system. You have the order in front of you and you look at it while your partner gives you the information that he or she has about your order. Listen to your partner and either confirm or correct the information that he or she gives you.

Bestellschein

Kleidungsartikel	Katalognummer/ Seite	Größe	Farbe	Menge (*quantity*)	Preis
Minirock	13, S. 70	32	schwarz	1	€12,50
Ohrringe	104, S. 23	—	gold	2 Paar	€17,50 (x2)
Handtasche	152, S. 30	—	braun	1	€22,50
Hut	20, S. 15	L	grau	1	€15,00
Mütze	22, S. 16	L	rot, blau und weiß	2	€7,50 (x2)

Communicative Activity 1-3 A

a. You and a friend (your partner) are planning a surprise party for a mutual friend, but you are having difficulty finding a time when everyone is free. Each of you called several friends to find out their weekend plans, and now you are exchanging information about the people with whom you spoke. First, ask your partner what the people listed below have planned, and then answer your partner's questions. When you have all the information, decide on the best time for the surprise party.

Name	Pläne	Wann?	Um wie viel Uhr?
Christian			
Annette			
Andreas			
Georg			
Ulrike			

b. Your partner would like to know about the plans of the people with whom you spoke, so that the two of you can figure out when to have the party. Use the information in the chart below to answer your partner's questions.

Name	Pläne	Wann?	Um wie viel Uhr?
Michael	geht mit seiner Freundin ins Kino	Samstagnachmittag	von 2 bis 5 Uhr
Sandra	muss zu Hause helfen	Samstag, den ganzen Tag	von 9 bis 4 Uhr
Paula	geht einkaufen	Samstagmorgen	schon um 8 Uhr
Monika	geht ins Konzert	Sonntagabend	von 8 bis 10 Uhr
Gabi	muss auf ihre Schwester aufpassen	Sonntagnachmittag	von 3 bis 5 Uhr

Communicative Activity 1-3 B

a. You and a friend (your partner) are planning a surprise party for a mutual friend, but you are having difficulty finding a time when everyone is free. Each of you called several friends to find out their weekend plans, and now you are exchanging information about the people with whom you spoke. Your partner will ask you about the plans of the people listed below, and then he or she will answer your questions. When you have all the information, decide on the best time to have the surprise party.

Name	Pläne	Wann?	Um wie viel Uhr?
Christian	geht mit seinem Vetter in den Zoo	Samstagnachmittag	um 1 Uhr 30
Annette	geht Schlittschuh laufen	Samstagmorgen	von 8 bis 12 Uhr
Andreas	ist müde und will nur faulenzen	Samstag, den ganzen Tag	um 8 Uhr—und 9 Uhr —und 10 Uhr, usw.!
Georg	geht auf eine Fete	Freitagabend	von 8 bis 10 Uhr
Ulrike	muss ihrem Bruder bei seinen Hausaufgaben helfen	Sonntagnachmittag	von 4 bis 6 Uhr

b. Now find out about the people with whom your partner spoke. Ask your partner questions about the people's plans and jot down the information you receive. Use all the facts you have gathered to make a decision about the best time to have the surprise party.

Name	Pläne	Wann?	Um wie viel Uhr?
Michael			
Sandra			
Paula			
Monika			
Gabi			

Holt German 2 Komm mit!, Chapter 1

COMMUNICATIVE ACTIVITIES

Communicative Activity 2-1 A

a. Who didn't take out the garbage? In the Müller family everyone helps with the house-work. But whoever is responsible for emptying the trash neglected to do it, because now they can't find the garbage can, hidden as it is behind piles of trash. Because Frau Müller understandably has a hard time remembering the tasks of all six of her children, she asks Herr Müller, who has a photographic memory, to tell her their chore responsi-bilities so she can write them down in order to keep better track. Play the role of Frau Müller and ask your partner, who plays the role of Herr Müller, to provide you with the missing information. Who was the garbage can culprit?

BEISPIEL **Was ist Dieters Aufgabe?**
Was soll Jana tun?

Familienmitglieder:

Franz	
Dieter	
Hans	
Jana	
Claudia	
Sabine	
Martin	

b. A similar case occurred in another family. This time, whoever was supposed to dust didn't do it. The father, Herr Borstenmeyer, is already complaining that he cannot watch TV anymore because of the dust layer. You are Frau Borstenmeyer. With the help of the chart below, provide your partner with the information he or she needs.

Familienmitglieder:

Erik	Rasen mähen
Janett	Wäsche waschen
Thomas	Müll wegtragen
Tara	in der Küche helfen
Katrin	Fußboden putzen
Claus	Auto polieren
Susanne	Staub wischen

COMMUNICATIVE ACTIVITIES

Communicative Activity 2-1 B

a. Who didn't take out the garbage? In the Müller family everyone helps with the house-work. But whoever is responsible for emptying the trash neglected to do it, because now they can't find the garbage can, hidden as it is behind piles of trash. Because Frau Müller understandably has a hard time remembering the tasks of all six of her children, she asks Herr Müller, who has a photographic memory, to tell her their chore responsi-bilities so she can write them down in order to keep better track. Your partner acts as Frau Müller and asks you, Herr Müller, about each person's chore. With the help of the chart, respond to your partner's questions.

BEISPIEL   **Franz soll ...**
            Dieter soll ...

Familienmitglieder:

Franz	Auto polieren
Dieter	Auto putzen
Hans	Garage aufräumen
Jana	Wäsche waschen
Claudia	Wäsche trocknen und bügeln
Sabine	Staub wischen
Martin	Müll wegtragen

b. A similar case occurred in another family. This time, whoever was supposed to dust didn't do it. You, Herr Borstenmeyer (the father), are already complaining that you can-not watch TV anymore because of the dust layer. Find out who is supposed to do what around the house by asking your partner and filling in the chart below. Who was guilty of letting the dust collect?

Familienmitglieder:

Erik	
Janett	
Thomas	
Tara	
Katrin	
Claus	
Susanne	

Communicative Activity 2-2 A

a. You are the owner of a store that sells jewelry, watches, and radios. You want to give a gift certificate (**einen Gutschein**) worth €50 to customers who spend at least €250 on products in the store. But don't tell them your plan! Your partner will play the roles of three customers in your store. Ask each what he or she wants to buy and tell that person how much each item costs. Then add up each person's purchases and decide who gets the gift certificate. Tell that person why. Remember to use formal address. Here's your inventory:

Ring aus Gold mit Diamanten — €179
Ring aus Gold — €139
Ring aus Silber — €112
Halskette mit Perle — €89
Halskette — €74
Radio mit Kassettenspieler — €41
Radio — €34
Wecker mit Radio und LED Anzeige — €26
Wecker mit Radio — €43
Wecker — €19

Herr _____: _____

_____

_____

Frau _____: _____

_____

_____

Frau _____: _____

_____

_____

b. Now you get to play the roles of three high-school students who have heard about a secret bonus being given out at a sporting goods store. Your partner is the owner of the store and wants to know what each of you would like to buy. Who will be the winner?

Michael:
ein Paar Stich Tennisschuhe;
zwei Jugend-Fußbälle;
einen Graf Tennisschläger;
eine Sporthose

Klaus:
zwei Agassi Tennisschläger;
zwei Sporthosen;
einen Profi-Fußball;
ein Paar Becker Tennisschuhe

Andrea:
nur eine Sporthose;
und zwei Profi-Fußbälle

Communicative Activity 2-2 B

a. You will play the roles of three customers who enter a store that sells jewelry, radios, and watches. The salesclerk will ask what each customer wants to buy, saying how much each item costs. Respond using the information below. Afterwards, the salesclerk will have a surprise for one customer.

Herr Pöckelbock:
einen Ring aus Gold;
eine Halskette;
einen Wecker mit Radio
    und LED Anzeige

Frau Mittelstrumpf:
einen Ring aus Silber;
ein Radio;
eine Halskette mit Perle;
einen Wecker

Frau Wanglierig:
einen Ring aus Gold mit
    Diamanten;
ein Radio mit Kassettenspieler;
einen Wecker mit Radio

b. Now you are the owner of a sporting goods store. Because the soccer World Cup tournament is coming up, you want to give out a gift certificate (**einen Gutschein**) worth €25 to the customer who spends the most on soccer balls. But don't tell your customers your plan! Ask each customer what he or she wants to buy and tally up the information. At the end, give the gift certificate to the appropriate customer and explain the reason for the gift. Here's your inventory:

Graf Tennisschläger — €114
Agassi Tennisschläger — €135
Becker Tennisschuhe — €137
Stich Tennisschuhe — €64
Profi-Fußball — €43
Jugend-Fußball — €35
Sporthose — €40

Michael: _____
_____
_____
_____

Klaus: _____
_____
_____
_____

Andrea: _____
_____
_____
_____

Name _____ Klasse _____ Datum _____

a. You're an exchange student in Germany. You and your host sibling have been sent out to buy groceries for your host family, several members of which have decided to hold an impromptu cooking contest.

You have been sent out to the baker's and the fresh produce store. Unfortunately, you brought with you the list that your host sibling needs. (He or she has been sent to the supermarket and the butcher's.) Because you are both in a hurry to buy the groceries and take them back home in time for the contest, you call your host sibling on the cell phone **(das Handy)** to find out what you need to buy. Quiz your partner in order to fill in the blanks below.

BEISPIEL   DU **Was soll ich zuerst kaufen?**
        PARTNER **Kauf dem Opa 1 kg Zwiebeln im Supermarkt!**

Was?	Wie viel?	Wem?	Wo?

b. Now answer your host sibling's questions about the purchases he or she needs to make, based on the information provided below.

        1 Pfd. Kartoffeln, Tante Hannelore, Supermarkt
        200 g Aufschnitt, Onkel Markus, Metzger
        5 Pfirsiche, Oma, Supermarkt
        1 Pfd. Bananen, Oma, Supermarkt
        150 g Leberkäs, Markus, Metzger
        250 g grüne Bohnen, Hannelore, Supermarkt

When you and your host sibling return home, you find that Tante Hannelore and Oma have both fallen sick with a stomach bug! You take Hannelore's ingredients and whip up a dish of your own. Think of a German name for your dish, and describe below (in English) how you'll combine the ingredients to create this award-winning example of your culinary talent.

_____

_____

_____

COMMUNICATIVE ACTIVITIES

 Communicative Activity 2-3 B

a. You're a German teenager, and your family is hosting an exchange student from the United States. You and your guest have been sent out to buy groceries for your family, several members of which have decided to hold an impromptu cooking contest.

You have been sent out to the supermarket and the butcher's. Unfortunately, you brought with you the list that your guest needs. (He or she has been sent to the baker's and the fresh produce store.) Because you are both in a hurry to buy the groceries and take them back home in time for the contest, you talk to your partner on the cell phone **(das Handy)** in order to find out what each of you needs to buy. Using the information provided below, answer your guest's questions.

BEISPIEL   PARTNER **Was soll ich zuerst kaufen?**
                  DU **Kauf dem Opa 1 kg Zwiebeln im Supermarkt!**

300 g Erbsen, Tante Hannelore, im Obst- und Gemüseladen
5 Brötchen, Onkel Markus, Bäcker
250 g Zwetschgen, Oma, im Obst- und Gemüseladen
6 Semmeln, Markus, Bäcker
2 kg Trauben, Oma, im Obst- und Gemüseladen
100 g Spinat, Hannelore, im Obst- und Gemüseladen

b. Now it's your turn to ask your partner questions about the items you need to purchase. Quiz your partner to fill in the blanks below.

Was?	Wie viel?	Wem?	Wo?

When you and your host sibling return home, you find that Tante Hannelore and Oma have both fallen sick with a stomach bug! You take Oma's ingredients and whip up a dish of your own. Think of a German name for your dish, and describe below (in English) how you'll combine the ingredients to create this award-winning example of your culinary talent.

_____

_____

_____

Holt German 2 Komm mit!, Chapter 2

Communicative Activity 3-1 A

a. You just returned from a one-week vacation to Germany. Unfortunately, you bumped your head on the airplane as you returned to the United States, and have forgotten many of the entertaining experiences you had while there. Fortunately, however, your partner was on the trip with you, and can tell you all about the time spans which you have forgotten. Quiz your partner in order to fill in the blanks below.

> BEISPIEL   DU   **Was habe ich am Montagvormittag gemacht?**
>   PARTNER   **Du bist Wasserski gelaufen.**

am Sonntagnachmittag?

Ich _____

am Montagabend?

Ich _____

am Dienstagvormittag?

Ich _____

am Mittwochabend?

Ich _____

am Donnerstagnachmittag?

Ich _____

am Freitagvormittag?

Ich _____

am Samstagabend?

Ich _____

b. As you were working on your car, a friend startled you and caused you to hit your head again, this time on the car hood. When you recovered consciousness, you realized that your memory had returned! Now you have to help your partner, who had an unfortunate run-in with a tree limb, remember what he or she did while on vacation. Use the conversational past to answer your partner's questions, based on the information provided below.

> **Sonntagvormittag: nach Berlin fahren**
> **Montagnachmittag: das Rote Rathaus besichtigen**
> **Dienstagabend: zu viel Mineralwasser trinken**
> **Mittwochnachmittag: um den See schwimmen**
> **Donnerstagvormittag: einen Ausflug nach Potsdam machen**
> **Freitagabend: ein Stück der Mauer kaufen**
> **Samstagnachmittag: der Tante beim Kochen helfen**

Communicative Activity 3-1 B

a. You and your partner just returned from a vacation in Germany. Unfortunately, he or she has forgotten much of what happened during the trip due to a run-in with the airplane door. Since you stayed together most of the time you were there, you can remind your partner about all the entertaining experiences he or she had. Use the conversational past to answer your partner's questions, based on the information provided below.

BEISPIEL   PARTNER **Was habe ich am Montagvormittag gemacht?**
                       DU **Du bist Wasserski gelaufen.**

> **Sonntagnachmittag:** Musik hören
> **Montagabend:** ins Kino gehen
> **Dienstagvormittag:** Leberkäs mit Senf essen
> **Mittwochabend:** Schach mit dem Weltmeister spielen
> **Donnerstagnachmittag:** im Hotel bleiben
> **Freitagvormittag:** in den Bergen wandern
> **Samstagabend:** das Buch *Der Zauberberg* lesen

b. Now it's your turn to quiz your partner. Being similarly accident-prone, you bumped your head on a tree limb right after returning to the United States, and are experiencing partial amnesia. Fortunately, though, you told your partner all about your experiences in Germany before your accident. Now he or she will answer your questions about what you did there. Use the information you receive to fill in the blanks below.

am Sonntagvormittag?

Ich _____

am Montagnachmittag?

Ich _____

am Dienstagabend?

Ich _____

am Mittwochnachmittag?

Ich _____

am Donnerstagvormittag?

Ich _____

am Freitagabend?

Ich _____

am Samstagnachmittag?

Ich _____

COMMUNICATIVE ACTIVITIES

Communicative Activity 3-2 A

a. A travel agency is giving away a trip to the winner of a contest. The topic of the contest is: How well do you know Germany?

There are three finalists who are now into the last two rounds of the contest. The one with the most correct answers is the winner of the first round. Who is it? In order to decide who the winner is, you have to fill in the chart below. Your partner has the information you need. Find out from your partner what answers were given by the people on your list. Then you can decide who has the highest number of correct answers. This person is the winner of the first round.

The questions in the first round were:
1. **Wo liegt die Stadt Dresden?**
2. **Wo ist das Goethehaus (Geburtshaus von Goethe)?**
3. **Welche Stadt hat keinen Zoo?**
4. **Welche Stadt liegt in den Bergen?**

	Antwort auf Frage 1	Antwort auf Frage 2	Antwort auf Frage 3	Antwort auf Frage 4
Rolf Hermann				
Hans Müller				
Rita Weiße				

b. Will your winner in the first round also be the winner of the second round? Find out together with your partner. This time, your partner will ask you the questions and you will provide the information that he or she needs. [Correct answers are shown in the chart in *italics*.]

Questions in Round 2:
1. **Wo ist die Marienkirche?**
2. **Welche Stadt hat keinen Dom?**
3. **Wo ist der Zwinger?**
4. **Was ist der Römer, und wo ist er?**

	Antwort auf Frage 1	Antwort auf Frage 2	Antwort auf Frage 3	Antwort auf Frage 4
Rolf Hermann	Berlin	Köln	Frankfurt	die Kirche in Frankfurt
Hans Müller	Stuttgart	Frankfurt	*Dresden*	ein Museum in Dresden
Rita Weiße	*Dresden*	*St. Ulrich*	Berlin	*das Rathaus in Frankfurt*

Name _____ Klasse _____ Datum _____

Communicative Activity 3-2 B

a. A travel agency is giving away a trip to the winner of a contest. The topic of the contest is: How well do you know Germany?

There are three finalists who are now into the last two rounds of the contest. The one with the most correct answers is the winner of the first round. Who is it? You listened to the first round and have the answers that were given by the contestants. Your partner will ask you questions to find out how the first round turned out. The person in each round who has the highest number of correct answers is the winner. [Correct answers are shown in the chart in *italics*.]

Questions in the first round were:
1. **Wo liegt die Stadt Dresden?**
2. **Wo ist das Goethehaus (Geburtshaus von Goethe)?**
3. **Welche Stadt hat keinen Zoo?**
4. **Welche Stadt liegt in den Bergen?**

	Antwort auf Frage 1	Antwort auf Frage 2	Antwort auf Frage 3	Antwort auf Frage 4
Rolf Hermann	am Main	*in Frankfurt*	Berlin	Frankfurt
Hans Müller	*an der Elbe*	in Berlin	*St. Ulrich*	*St. Ulrich*
Rita Weiße	an der Saale	in Stuttgart	Frankfurt	Berlin

b. Will the winner from the first round also be the winner of the second round? Find out together with your partner. This time, you have to ask the questions in order to fill in the chart. Then you can discover with your partner who the winner of the second round is.

Questions for the second round were:
1. **Wo ist die Marienkirche?**
2. **Welche Stadt hat keinen Dom?**
3. **Wo ist der Zwinger?**
4. **Was ist der Römer, und wo ist er?**

	Antwort auf Frage 1	Antwort auf Frage 2	Antwort auf Frage 3	Antwort auf Frage 4
Rolf Hermann				
Hans Müller				
Rita Weiße				

Holt German 2 Komm mit!, Chapter 3

Name _____ Klasse _____ Datum _____

a. You work for a travel agency that arranges class trips for schools. You are conducting a survey about how the students liked their accommodations and which region they liked the best. (The students asked went on different class trips.) Ask your partner questions to complete the chart below. Your partner will take the role of the students and provide you with the answers. Which region or town made the best impression on the students surveyed?

	Wo bist du gewesen?	Wo hast du übernachtet?	Wo hast du Frühstück/Abend-brot gegessen?	Wie war das Essen?
Jana				
Michaela				
Anke				

b. Your partner works for a travel agency and asks three other students about their class trip. Your partner's questions are slightly different from yours, but all the questions together are designed to give you a clear picture about what the students liked best about their trips. Play the role of the students below, using the information from the chart to answer your partner's questions.

	Wo bist du gewesen?	Wie hat dir die Stadt gefallen?	Wie hat es dir in der Oper gefallen?	Was hast du am liebsten gemacht?
Sara	Leipzig	phantastisch	echt super	spazieren gehen
Paul	Frankfurt	nicht besonders	na ja, soso	Museen besuchen
Elke	Berlin	na ja, soso	wahnsinnig gut	fotografieren

COMMUNICATIVE ACTIVITIES

 Communicative Activity 3-3 B

a. Your partner works for a travel agency that arranges class trips for schools. He or she wants to find out how the students interviewed liked their accommodations and which region they liked the best. Using the chart below, play the role of the students and give the agent the information requested.

	Wo bist du gewesen?	Wo hast du übernachtet?	Wo hast du Frühstück/Abend- brot gegessen?	Wie war das Essen?
Jana	Frankfurt	Hotel	Frühstück und Abendbrot im Hotel	phantastisch
Michaela	Berlin	Jugendherberge	Frühstück in der Jugendherberge, Abendbrot im Restaurant	Frühstück nicht besonders, Abendbrot gut
Anke	Dresden	Pension	Frühstück und Abendbrot im Gasthof	na ja, soso

b. Now it's your turn to be the travel agent. Ask your partner the questions from the chart below to find out which region or town got the most positive response from the students being surveyed.

	Wo bist du gewesen?	Wie hat dir die Stadt gefallen?	Wie hat es dir in der Oper gefallen?	Was hast du am liebsten gemacht?
Sara				
Paul				
Elke				

Communicative Activity 4-1 A

a. You and your partner are both working for the school paper. You want to write an article on students' lifestyles. You have already conducted the interviews, and the notes you took can be seen below. You each focused on different aspects of lifestyle, and now you have to get information from each other in order to compile it and obtain a complete picture. Your interviews contain information about how the students interviewed feel in general and which, if any, sports or other physical activities they do. Your partner will ask you questions in order to get that information.

INTERVIEWS:

Manuela: Ich fühle mich meistens gut. Das liegt vielleicht daran, dass ich jeden Morgen jogge und am Wochenende immer schwimme.

Carola: Ich finde es toll, dass es bei uns an der Schule einen Gymnastikclub gibt. Dort mache ich viel Gymnastik. Ich gehe zwar nicht jeden Morgen joggen, nur manchmal am Wochenende. Trotzdem fühle ich mich meistens großartig.

Dieter: Ich spiele in einer Fußballmannschaft, und dadurch bin ich ziemlich fit. Ich muss sagen, ich fühle mich ganz wohl.

b. Your partner gathered information from these same students about their eating, sleeping, and other habits. Ask your partner questions in order to get this information, so that you can include it in the final version of the article. Write the information you receive in the chart below.

	Wie viele Stunden schläfst du?	Was isst du?	Was machst du sonst für die Gesundheit?
Manuela			
Carola			
Dieter			

Communicative Activity 4-1 B

a. You and your partner are both working for the school paper. You want to write an article on students' lifestyles. You have already conducted the interviews, and the notes you took can be seen below. You each focused on different aspects of lifestyle, and now you have to get information from each other in order to compile it and obtain a complete picture. Your interviews contain information about how much the students sleep, what they eat, and any other facts about their health habits that you need for the article. Your partner will ask you questions in order to get that information. First, however, ask your partner questions about how the students feel and in what sports or other activities they participate.

	Wie fühlt sich ...?	Welchen Sport oder welche anderen Tätigkeiten macht ...?
Manuela		
Carola		
Dieter		

b. Now your partner will ask you about the interviews you conducted. They are given below and will provide your partner with all the information needed to get a complete picture of these students' lifestyles.

INTERVIEWS:

Manuela: Ich schlafe nicht viel, aber ich esse richtig: ich esse viel Obst und Gemüse und wenig Fleisch. Ich fühle mich im Allgemeinen wohl, vielleicht auch, weil ich keinen Alhohol trinke und die Sonne vermeide.

Carola: Ich rauche nicht. Ich esse viel Obst. Oft esse ich aber Schokolade. Ich weiß, dass das nicht sehr vernünftig ist. Schlafen? Mm — Schlaf ist mir ziemlich wichtig. Ich schlafe nachts mindestens sieben Stunden.

Dieter: Genügend schlafen, das ist für mich das Wichtigste. Ich schlafe selten weniger als acht Stunden. Ich rauche nicht, ich trinke auch nicht, aber ich esse auch nicht immer richtig — ich esse nicht viel Obst, zum Beispiel, sondern lieber Fleisch. Trotzdem fühle ich mich ganz wohl.

Communicative Activity 4-2 A

a. You are a salesperson in a grocery store and your partner is your assistant. For purposes of future planning, you need to know what products your customers buy and how often they buy them. Your assistant keeps track of such things and can give you that information. Ask him or her about the products shown in the chart. Fill in the chart. Then, together with your assistant, make a list of the products and suggested amounts that should be ordered for the coming month.

BEISPIEL   DU **Wie oft kaufen unsere Kunden Brokkoli?**

Brokkoli	
Blumenkohl	
Möhren	
Pilze	
Erdbeeren	
Aprikosen	
Kirschen	
Blaubeeren	

b. This time you are the shop owner, and you just came back from a meeting with marketing experts. There has been extensive research on why people buy certain products more often than others. The salesperson wants to know about that and asks you for this information. (NOTE: When you are giving reasons, begin your answer with **weil**).

Eis	selten	zu viel Zucker
Joghurt	oft	wenig Kalorien
Forelle	oft	gesund
Karpfen	selten	hat zu viel Fett
Huhn	selten	zu viele Kalorien
Rindfleisch	selten	nicht gut für die Gesundheit

COMMUNICATIVE ACTIVITIES

Communicative Activity 4-2 B

a. You are a shop assistant in a store, and your partner is one of the salespersons. Your partner needs to know what products your customers buy and how often they buy them. Give him or her the information from the chart.

Brokkoli	sehr oft
Blumenkohl	selten
Möhren	normalerweise nicht so oft
Pilze	gewöhnlich sehr oft
Erdbeeren	sehr oft
Aprikosen	selten
Kirschen	nicht sehr oft
Blaubeeren	sehr selten

b. Your partner, the shop owner, has been to a marketing conference and has learned a great deal about why people buy certain products and why they don't buy others. You have already learned how often these products are purchased, but you need to know the reasons why. You ask the owner to share this information with you. Ask about the products in the chart below and fill in the information that you receive.

BEISPIEL   DU **Warum kaufen unsere Kunden eigentlich so selten Rindfleisch?**

Eis	selten	
Joghurt	oft	
Forelle	oft	
Karpfen	selten	
Huhn	selten	
Rindfleisch	selten	

Communicative Activity 4-3 A

a. You're interested in getting your partner's opinion about some of your health habits. Using the prompts in the first column of the table below, tell your partner about something you do. He or she will express approval or disapproval of your statement; you should put a check mark in the appropriate box. If your partner disapproves, he or she should then give you advice about what you should do differently. Record the advice in the last column.

BEISPIEL   DU **Ich esse jeden Tag Pommes frites.**
       PARTNER **Ich finde es nicht gut, dass du so oft Pommes frites isst. Die sollst du nur selten essen.**

Gewohnheit (habit)	Billigung? (approval)	Missbilligung? (disapproval)	Rat (advice)
jede Woche ein bisschen Brokkoli essen			
nicht viel lesen			
sehr spät ins Bett gehen			
dreimal die Woche fechten			
viel Sahne essen			
jedes Obst gern haben			
jedes Wochenende wandern			
keine Schokolade essen			
ziemlich viel in der Sonne sitzen			
nicht viel für die Gesundheit tun			

b. Now it's your turn to give your friend some advice. Respond appropriately to your partner's statements about his or her health habits. If you disapprove of an action, be sure to give your friend some advice about what he or she should do differently in the future.

Communicative Activity 4-3 B

a. Your partner will tell you about a few of his or her habits and attitudes. You should respond by expressing either approval or disapproval. If you disapprove of an action or opinion, be sure to give your partner some advice about what he or she should do differently in the future.

BEISPIEL   PARTNER   **Ich esse jeden Tag Pommes frites.**
               DU   **Ich finde es nicht gut, dass du so oft Pommes frites isst. Die sollst du nur selten essen.**

b. Now it's your turn to solicit your partner's opinions about your own health habits. Using the prompts in the first column of the table below, tell your partner about something you do. He or she will express approval or disapproval of your statement; you should put a check mark in the appropriate box. If your partner disapproves, he or she should then give you advice about what you should do differently. Record the advice in the last column.

Gewohnheit (habit)	Billigung? (approval)	Missbilligung? (disapproval)	Rat (advice)
normalerweise kein Gemüse essen			
in einer Fußballmannschaft sein			
nicht rauchen			
jeden Tag Kaffee trinken			
keine Beeren essen			
regelmäßig Sport machen			
ziemlich oft fernsehen			
viel Butter essen			
Vollkornsemmeln gern haben			
sich meistens sehr wohl fühlen			

COMMUNICATIVE ACTIVITIES

Communicative Activity 5-1 A

a. You and your friend are the new editors of the nutrition page for your school newspaper. You are about to do an article on "the sandwich," so you want to find out from several students what kinds of sandwiches they like best. You interviewed four students, and your partner interviewed four others. Put all the information together and draw some conclusions about the most popular and the least popular sandwiches.

Your partner will ask you about the students you interviewed. Share the information below with him or her.

	Monika	Tara	Jan	Mike
Was für Brot?	dunkles	helles	Brötchen	dunkles
Mayonnaise?				
Senf?				
Butter?	✔		✔	
Margarine?				
Käse?	✔		✔	
Was für Käse?	Tilsiter		Schweizer	
Schinken?				
Was für Aufschnitt?	Leberwurst			
Tomaten?	✔			✔
Kopfsalat?	✔			
Marmelade?		✔		
Erdnussbutter?		✔		
Tofu?				✔
Sojasprossen?			✔	✔

b. Now your partner will answer your questions about the students listed below. When you have finished, answer the questions that follow.

	Manuela	Heiko	Frank	Gabi
Was für Brot?				
Mayonnaise?				
Senf?				
Butter?				
Margarine?				
Käse?				
Was für Käse?				
Schinken?				
Was für Aufschnitt?				
Tomaten?				
Kopfsalat?				
Marmelade?				
Erdnussbutter?				
Tofu?				
Sojasprossen?				

1. What is the most popular type of sandwich? _____

2. What is the least popular type of sandwich? _____

COMMUNICATIVE ACTIVITIES

Communicative Activity 5-1 B

a. You and your friend are the new editors of the nutrition page for your school newspaper. You are about to do an article on "the sandwich," so you want to find out from several students what kinds of sandwiches they like best. You interviewed four students, and your partner interviewed four others. Put all the information together and draw some conclusions about the most popular and the least popular sandwiches.

Ask your partner about the students he or she interviewed.

	Monika	Tara	Jan	Mike
Was für Brot?				
Mayonnaise?				
Senf?				
Butter?				
Margarine?				
Käse?				
Was für Käse?				
Schinken?				
Was für Aufschnitt?				
Tomaten?				
Kopfsalat?				
Marmelade?				
Erdnussbutter?				
Tofu?				
Sojasprossen?				

b. Now your partner will ask you about the four students you interviewed. Share the information below with him or her. When you have finished, answer the two questions that follow.

	Manuela	Heiko	Frank	Gabi
Was für Brot?	dunkles	helles	helles	helles
Mayonnaise?	✔		✔	
Senf?				
Butter?		✔		
Margarine?				
Käse?	✔		✔	
Was für Käse?	Camembert		Tilsiter	
Schinken?				
Was für Aufschnitt?		Salami	Leberwurst	
Tomaten?		✔	✔	
Kopfsalat?		✔	✔	
Marmelade?				
Erdnussbutter?				
Tofu?				✔
Sojasprossen?	✔			✔

1. What is the most popular type of sandwich? _____

2. What is the least popular type of sandwich? _____

Communicative Activity 5-2 A

a. You are reading the menu at a new restaurant. When the waitperson comes to take your order, ask him or her about some of the food items on the menu and jot down the information in the chart below. Your partner is the waitperson.

You might ask him or her, for example,

> **Welche Suppe ist gut?**
>
> **Welches Gemüse gibt es/haben Sie?**

	gut	besser
Suppe		
Gemüse		
Fleisch		
Fisch		
Obst		
Nachtisch		

b. A friend of yours has just arrived to join you for dinner. He or she asks which dishes are particularly good. You try to tell him or her what you learned from the waitperson, but you can't remember everything. Use the information below to tell your friend what you recall, and have your friend take notes. Then compare these notes with what you wrote earlier when you talked to the waitperson. What mistakes did you make?

	gut	besser
Suppe	Brokkolisuppe	Blumenkohlsuppe
Gemüse	Blumenkohl	Sauerkraut
Fleisch	Rindersteak	Schweinefleisch
Fisch	Fischstäbchen	Forelle
Obst	Erdbeeren	Trauben
Nachtisch	Pflaumenkuchen	Käsekuchen

COMMUNICATIVE ACTIVITIES

 Communicative Activity 5-2 B

a. You are the waitperson in the restaurant where your partner is eating. He or she wants to know about certain food items on the menu. Give him or her advice about which items you think are good and which you think are better in your restaurant.

Say, for example,

Die Blumenkohlsuppe ist gut, aber die Brokkolisuppe ist besser.

	gut	**besser**
Suppe	Blumenkohlsuppe	Brokkolisuppe
Gemüse	Möhren	Sauerkraut
Fleisch	Rindersteak	Schnitzel
Fisch	Fischstäbchen	Heilbutt
Obst	Aprikosen	Trauben
Nachtisch	Käsekuchen	Pflaumenkuchen

b. You have just arrived at a new restaurant. Your partner arrived earlier and has gotten some information about which food items on the menu are good and which are better than others. Unfortunately, he or she cannot recall everything exactly and gives you some incorrect information. First get the information from your friend by asking questions. Then compare your notes with those taken by your friend earlier. What mistakes did your friend make?

You might ask, for example,

> **Welche Suppe ist gut?**
>
> or **Was haben sie/gibt es als Gemüse?**

	gut	**besser**
Suppe		
Gemüse		
Fleisch		
Fisch		
Obst		
Nachtisch		

Communicative Activity 5-3 A

a. Let's play **Kreuzworträtseln zu Zweit** (*Crossword Puzzle for Two*)! You have the items whose German equivalents fit into the **senkrecht** (*down*) positions of the puzzle. Your partner has the items whose German equivalents fit into the **waagrecht** (*across*) positions. Take turns in describing the food items in German. You go first. Once your partner guesses the "down" item correctly, you may fill his or her answer into the puzzle below; this may help you in guessing the items belonging in the "across" positions.

For example, for the item "mustard" you may say: **7, senkrecht. Er hat eine gelbe Farbe und man findet ihn auf dem Wurstbrot.**

senkrecht *(down):*

1. Er ist weich; er sieht aus wie Käse; er kommt von Sojabohnen (tofu)
2. Er ist ein Fisch; er lebt im See; er beginnt mit dem Buchstaben "K" (carp)
3. Man trinkt sie; sie hat eine weiße Farbe; sie kommt von der Kuh (milk)
4. Sie hat eine gelbe Farbe; sie kommt aufs Brot; sie ist aus Milch gemacht (butter)
5. Er hat eine gelbe oder weiße Farbe; er kommt oft aufs Brot oder auf Cracker (cheese)
6. Es ist aus Getreide; man isst Wurst und Käse darauf (bread)
7. *filled in to give example*
8. Sie ist ein Fisch; sie lebt im Meer und im See (trout)
9. Zum Beispiel: Äpfel, Bananen, Pfirsiche, Aprikosen (fruit)
10. Er ist ein Fisch; er lebt im Meer (halibut)
11. Zum Beispiel: Brokkoli, Blumenkohl, Möhren (vegetables)
12. Er ist weich und weiß; oft kommt er mit Früchten (yogurt)
13. Sie haben oft eine weiße Farbe und ein Käppi; einige sind giftig (mushrooms)
14. Sie ist eine Frucht; sie ist klein und rund; sie ist grün oder rot (grape)

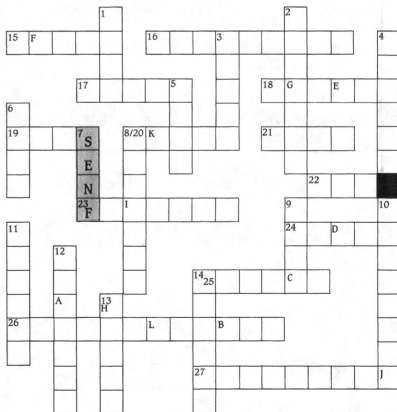

b. For extra credit, fill in below the letters from those boxes in the puzzle that are designated with small letters.

A	B	C	D	E		F	G	H	I	J	K	L

Name _____ Klasse _____ Datum _____

Communicative Activity 5-3 B

a. Let's play **Kreuzworträtseln zu Zweit** (*Crossword Puzzle for Two*)! You have the items whose German equivalents fit into the **waagrecht** (*across*) positions of the puzzle. Your partner has the items whose German equivalents fit into the **senkrecht** (*down*) positions. Take turns in describing the food items in German. Your partner will describe an item in the "down" position. After you have guessed this item, write it in the puzzle and then it's your turn to describe to your partner an item in the "across" position. You may put his or her answer in the puzzle below; this may help you in guessing the items belonging in the "down" positions.

For example, for the item "mustard" your partner may say: **7, senkrecht. Er hat eine gelbe Farbe und man findet ihn auf dem Wurstbrot.**

waagrecht *(across)*

15. Er ist zum Trinken; er hat eine braune Farbe und ist süß (chocolate milk)
16. Sie ist aus Früchten gemacht; sie ist süß; sie kommt aufs Brot (marmelade)
17. Er ist eine deutsche Spezialität; er ist weich; er sieht aus wie Käse; man isst ihn oft mit Schnittlauch (Quark)
18. Er ist ein Gemüse mit grüner Farbe; man findet ihn oft im Salat (spinach)
19. Das sind weiße Körner; er ist oft in chinesischen Gerichten (rice)
20. Er schwimmt im Meer (fish)
21. Es ist in Pommes frites; es macht dick (fat)
22. Man isst es im Eiscafé; es ist süß und kalt; es kommt oft mit Früchten (ice cream)
23. Zum Beispiel: Schweinsbraten, Hackfleisch; Vegetarier essen es nicht (meat)
24. Sie ist eine kleine, runde Frucht; sie ist süß (berry)
25. Sie ist ein Gemüse; sie ist rot und rund (tomato)
26. Er hat eine grüne Farbe; man findet ihn in Suppen; man isst ihn mit Quark (chives)
27. Es ist ein Gemüse; es ist ein Kraut; es ist nicht sauer; es ist blau (red cabbage)

b. For extra credit, fill in below the letters from those boxes in the puzzle that are designated with small letters.

A	B	C	D	E		F	G	H	I	J	K	L

Holt German 2 Komm mit!, Chapter 5

Communicative Activity 6-1 A

a. There must be an epidemic in your school! Several people were missing this morning in homeroom, and the teacher has asked you and a friend to call the homes of the missing students to find out what is wrong. Your partner called some of the students and you called the rest. Ask your partner questions and record the information in the chart below, so that the two of you can put together a report for the teacher.

	Was fehlt ihr/ihm?
Anke	
Michael	
Heike	
Ariane	
Uwe	

b. Now answer your partner's questions about the students whom you called. When you have information about all the students, work with your partner to create a report for the teacher who asked you to make the calls.

	Was fehlt ihr/ihm?
Torsten	Bauchschmerzen
Sandra	Halsschmerzen mit Fieber
Christian	Kopf- und Ohrenschmerzen
Georg	Zahnschmerzen
Francine	Rückenschmerzen

Communicative Activity 6-1 B

a. You and your partner were asked to call several missing students to find out why they weren't in class. You called some of them and the information you got is recorded in the chart below. Answer your partner's questions about the missing students, so that he or she can record the information.

	Was fehlt ihr/ihm?
Anke	Bauchschmerzen
Michael	Halsschmerzen
Heike	Ohrenschmerzen
Ariane	Zahnschmerzen
Uwe	Kopfschmerzen

b. Your partner has information about why the rest of the students were missing from school. Ask him or her questions and use the information you get to fill in the chart below. When you and your partner have all the information together, write a report for the teacher who asked you to make the calls.

	Was fehlt ihr/ihm?
Torsten	
Sandra	
Christian	
Georg	
Francine	

Holt German 2 Komm mit!, Chapter 6

Communicative Activity 6-2 A

a. You and your partner work for a travel magazine. For the summer edition, you decided to include two articles: one about sunburn and the importance of protecting one's skin from the sun, and one about important items to take along on your vacation. Your partner was responsible for doing the research on the first topic, and you have talked to several people about the second topic. Ask your partner questions to find out what the people he or she interviewed do in order to protect themselves from sunburn. Write the information you get in the chart below.

	Wie schützen sich die Leute vor Sonnenbrand?
Karin	
Michaela	
Claus	
Dieter	
Jens	

b. Now tell your partner what you learned from five students about the items they consider important to take along on vacation. Your partner will record the information in a chart. When you and your partner have all the information together, write the two articles for the travel magazine.

	wichtige Dinge im Urlaub
Jannette	Zahnpasta, Seife
Mike	Sonnenmilch
Kristin	Handcreme
Tara	Sonnencreme
Frank	Shampoo

Name _____ Klasse _____ Datum _____

 Communicative Activity 6-2 B

a. You and your partner are doing research for the summer edition of the travel magazine where both of you work. The topics of the two articles you plan to write are as follows: sunburn and the importance of protecting yourself from the sun, and important items to take along on your vacation. As part of the research, you interviewed five people. Your partner will now ask you questions about your interviews and will record in a chart the information you give him or her.

Wie schützen sich die Leute vor Sonnenbrand?	
Karin	einen Sonnenhut tragen
Michaela	Sonnenmilch mit hohem Lichtschutzfaktor benutzen
Claus	nur leichte Speisen essen
Dieter	die Sonne vermeiden
Jens	viel Wasser trinken

b. Now ask your partner what he or she learned from five people about the items they consider important to take along on vacation. Write the information in the chart, and then work with your partner to compose the two articles for the travel magazine.

wichtige Dinge im Urlaub	
Jannette	
Mike	
Kristin	
Tara	
Frank	

Name _____ Klasse _____ Datum _____

Communicative Activity 6-3 A

COMMUNICATIVE ACTIVITIES

a. Let's play **Zeig auf die richtige Antwort** (*Point to the right answer*)! Place your finger at the START position. Your partner will ask you a question and you will move your finger to the box which contains the answer; you may move to any box next to the box you are on (including diagonals). Read aloud the statement written in the box you choose. If you give the wrong answer, your partner will tell you and give you another chance. Once you are on the square with the right answer, your partner will ask you another question. After you have answered all your partner's questions, you will see how well you did. BEWARE! You are allowed only three wrong answers in this game. Viel Glück!

Sie ist mir zu fett und auch zu teuer. 1	Nein, das ist nicht gut für die Gesundheit! 2	START 3	Ja, ich mag gern Erdnussbutter. 4
Ich habe Husten und Schnupfen. 5	Ja, ich hab Kopfschmerzen. 6	Nein, morgen gehe ich ins Kino. 7	Ja, ich mag Blumenkohl und Möhren. 8
Nein, sie ist mir zu parfümiert. 9	Nein, ich bleibe zu Hause. 10	Ruf doch den Arzt an! 11	Ja, ich kann kaum schlucken. 12
Ich putze mir die Zähne. 13	Nein, ich hab mir den Knöchel verstaucht. 14	Ja, ich bin sehr müde. 15	Das Shampoo ist mir zu teuer. 16
Nein, ich benutze nur Sonnencreme mit hohem Lichtschutzfaktor. 17	Gut gespielt! 18	Ja, weil es gut ist für die Gesundheit. 19	Ja, ich trinke keinen Alkohol. 20

b. Now it's your turn to ask your partner questions, and he/she will travel the board starting from box 3. (Correct box numbers are in parentheses behind each question)

QUESTIONS:
1. Trinkst du Alkohol? (2)
2. Warum kaufst du nicht diese Handcreme? (1)
3. Was fehlt dir? (5)
4. Kommst du mit ins Kino? (10)
5. Ich habe furchtbare Bauchschmerzen. (11)
6. Hast du Halsweh? (12)
7. Kaufst du dieses parfümierte Shampoo? (16)
8. Willst du eine Pause machen? (15)
9. Du hast beim Tennisspielen gewonnen. (18)

***For extra credit: Ask a question which has the statement in box 4 as answer.

Holt German 2 Komm mit!, Chapter 6   Activities for Communication **35**

Communicative Activity 6-3 B

a. Let's play **Zeig auf die richtige Antwort** (*Point to the right answer*)! It is your task to guide your partner from box 3 to the bottom row of the board by asking him or her the questions below. Your partner will move his or her finger to the box which contains the answer and read the answer aloud; he or she may move to any box next to the square he or she is on (including diagonals). If your partner answers question 1 correctly, he or she will move to box 8. If your partner moves to a box with a wrong answer, you may give him or her another chance. However, do not give your partner more than 3 chances during the game! Once on box 8, ask your partner question 2 and your partner should give the answer written in box 7. (Correct box numbers are in parentheses behind each question.)

QUESTIONS:
1. Isst du gern Gemüse? (8)
2. Kommst du morgen mit in die Stadt? (7)
3. Tut dir der Kopf weh? (6)
4. Kaufst du die Seife? (9)
5. Was tust du nach dem Essen? (13)
6. Kaufst du diese Sonnencreme? (17)
7. Hast du dir den Fuß gebrochen? (14)
8. Trinkst du viel Wasser? (19)
9. Wenn du hier bist, dann hast du wie gespielt? (18)

Sie ist mir zu fett und auch zu teuer. 1	Nein, das ist nicht gut für die Gesundheit! 2	**START** 3	Ja, ich mag gern Erdnussbutter. 4
Ich habe Husten und Schnupfen. 5	Ja, ich hab Kopfschmerzen. 6	Nein, morgen gehe ich ins Kino. 7	Ja, ich mag Blumenkohl und Möhren. 8
Nein, sie ist mir zu parfümiert. 9	Nein, ich bleibe zu Hause. 10	Ruf doch den Arzt an! 11	Ja, ich kann kaum schlucken. 12
Ich putze mir die Zähne. 13	Nein, ich hab mir den Knöchel ver-staucht. 14	Ja, ich bin sehr müde. 15	Das Shampoo ist mir zu teuer. 16
Nein, ich benutze nur Sonnencreme mit hohem Lichtschutzfaktor. 17	Gut gespielt! 18	Ja, weil es gut ist für die Gesundheit. 19	Ja, ich trinke keinen Alkohol. 20

b. Now it's your turn to travel the board. Your partner will ask you questions and you will answer aloud and move your finger to the box containing the answer you gave. Start from box 3 and don't forget that you are only allowed three strikes. Viel Glück!

***For extra credit: Ask a question which has the statement in box 20 as answer.

COMMUNICATIVE ACTIVITIES

Communicative Activity 7-1 A

a. You, a realtor at a real estate agency, receive a call from a potential customer. Take notes while listening to her description of her lifestyle. Then describe for her the houses you have on the market. Try to sell her each one, explaining what the advantages of that particular house are.

interessierte Käuferin: _____

sie mag	mag nicht
_____	_____
_____	_____
_____	_____
_____	_____

Unsere Firma hat folgende Häuser auf dem Markt:
1) „Friedrichsruh": in einem Dorf; große Küche; ruhige Nachbarn; kleine Geschäfte im nächsten Dorf
2) „Am Stadttor 15": öffentliche Verkehrsmittel in der Nähe; ruhige Nachbarschaft; sechs Zimmer; große Küche
3) „Marktstraße 12a": kleine, ältere Küche; viele Geschäfte in der Nähe; Autogarage; Bushaltestelle um die Ecke

BEISPIEL   **Also Frau** _____ **, ich glaube, dass ...**

b. Now switch roles. You, Herr Gruber, are a potential house buyer and call a real estate agency to see if they have anything appropriate for you. Introduce yourself and give them a short description of your lifestyle using the information below. Then listen to the realtor's recommendations. Take notes on what the agency is offering and express your preferences and reservations when necessary. After you've heard what the agency has to offer, decide which of the houses best suits you and justify your choice.

Herr Gruber, interessierter Käufer.

habe gern
wandern
im Garten arbeiten

habe nicht gern
moderne Dinge
viele Menschen
laute Nachbarn
schlechte Luft

Activities for Communication **37**

COMMUNICATIVE ACTIVITIES

Communicative Activity 7-1 B

a. You, Frau Hofmann, are a potential house buyer and call a real estate agency to see if they have anything appropriate for you. Introduce yourself and give them a short description of your lifestyle, using the information below. Then listen to the realtor's recommendations. Take notes on what the agency is offering and express your preferences and reservations when necessary. After you've heard what the agency has to offer, decide which of the houses best suits you and justify your choice.

Frau Hofmann, interessierte Käuferin.

habe gern	habe nicht gern
ausgehen	weit weg von Freunden sein
teure Kleidung	Auto fahren
Partys mit vielen Freunden	
lange aufbleiben	
kochen	

b. Now switch roles. You, a realtor at a real estate agency, receive a call from a potential customer. Take notes while listening to his description of his lifestyle. Then describe for him the houses you have on the market. Try to sell him each one, explaining what the advantages of that particular house are.

interessierter Käufer: _____

er mag	mag nicht
_____	_____
_____	_____
_____	_____
_____	_____
_____	_____

Häuser auf dem Markt:
1) „Am Stadtrand 11": netter Garten; U-Bahn Haltestelle vor dem Haus; schöne, alte Möbel; ganz nah an der Autobahn
2) „Hauptstraße 52": viele Geschäfte in der Nähe; toller Kinderpool im großen Garten; öffentliche Verkehrsmittel nicht weit
3) „Am Waldweg": auf dem Land; neue, moderne Möbel; saubere Luft; friedliche Nachbarschaft

BEISPIEL   **Also Herr** _____ **, ich glaube, dass ...**

Communicative Activity 7-2 A

a. You and your partner work for a gossipy German tabloid. The boss has sent both of you to a soirée at movie star Arnold Schwarzenegger's villa. You have a look around Arnold's house to get a description of the place, and your partner happens to cast a glance in Arnold's diary (**Tagebuch**) lying out on a table in the corner. First find out about Arnold's diary, and then share your information with your partner about Arnold's house. Of course, your sketch was done in a hurry, so you'll now have to provide the correct adjective endings.

BEISPIEL   DU **Was steht in Arnolds Tagebuch?**
        PARTNER **Hier steht, ...**
and then:
        PARTNER **Wie sehen Arnolds Haus und Garten aus?**
            DU **Er hat ...**

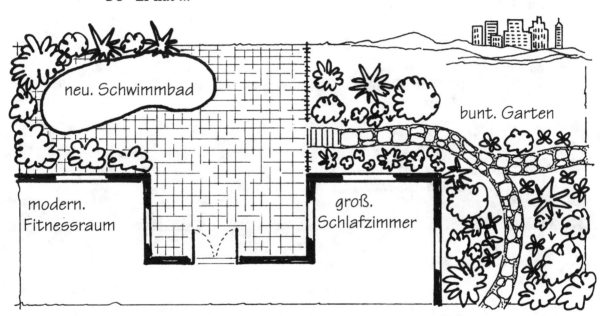

neu. Schwimmbad

bunt. Garten

modern. Fitnessraum

groß. Schlafzimmer

b. You must now write a short article describing for your readers what Arnold's life is like, his preferences, and his wishes for the future. Speculate on what Arnold probably feels the advantages and disadvantages of his life are.

COMMUNICATIVE ACTIVITIES

 Communicative Activity 7-2 B

a. You and your partner work for a gossipy German tabloid. The boss has sent both of you to a soirée at movie star Arnold Schwarzenegger's villa. You happen to get a glance at Arnold's diary **(Tagebuch)** lying out on a table in the corner, while your partner has a look around Arnold's house to get a description of the place. First tell your partner what you found out about Arnold's diary, and then find out from your partner what Arnold's house looks like.

Here are the quick notes you took while glancing through Arnold's diary. You'll have to add the adjective endings now!

„Ich wünsche mir ein kleines Haus auf dem Land ..."
... ein ruhig. Schlafz.
... hell. Flur
... älter. Esszimmer
... friedlich. Leben

and then:

          DU **Wie sehen Arnolds Haus und Garten aus?**
   PARTNER **Er hat ...**

b. You must now write a short article describing for your readers what Arnold's life is like, his preferences, and his wishes for the future. Speculate on what Arnold probably feels the advantages and disadvantages of his life are.

Name _____ Klasse _____ Datum _____

Communicative Activity 7-3 A

a. A big motion picture company has hired you to design the stage for the movie *Meine Familie*, which depicts the everyday life of a large family in Germany. In order to design an appropriate stage, you need to ask the **Regisseur** (stage director) for more information about this family. Make sure to take notes.

BEISPIEL   DU **Guten Tag! Darf ich Ihnen ein paar Fragen über**
***Meine Familie* stellen?**
REGISSEUR **Ja, natürlich.**
DU **Wie heißt diese Familie?**
REGISSEUR **Sie heißt Familie *Zahlreich*.**
DU **Wo wohnt diese Familie?**

You may also want to ask:

Where does the family live? In a town? In a village? In a suburb? In the mountains?
Why does the family want to live there? What is the advantage?
How many children does the family have? Sons? Daughters?
How old are the children and what are their names?
Does the family have a cat? A dog?
Does the family live in a house or an apartment?
How many rooms does their house have? How many bathrooms?
Does it have a cellar? A garden? A terrace? A pool?
Do the parents have a car? A motorcycle? Do the children have cars?
Do the parents have a good income? A good job? A good education?

Notes: _____

_____

_____

_____

_____

b. Now you are the stage director of the motion picture *Rex*, a movie about the excursions of a German shepherd. The stage designer asks you for more information about the movie and its characters in order to set up the appropriate stage.

You have the following information about this movie available:

The dog's name is Rex. He is black and 8 years old. He stays with Frau Babl, an older woman who lives in a small town. Her house is by the lake. Rex has a large garden with bushes and trees. His favorite meal is **Leberkäs**. *He likes to play with Mitzie, Frau Babl's cat. Since the older woman is blind, Rex works as* **Blindenhund** *(seeing-eye dog).*

Communicative Activity 7-3 B

a. You are the stage director of the motion picture *Meine Familie*, a movie about the every-day life of a large family in Germany. The stage designer asks you for more information about the movie and its characters in order to set up the appropriate stage.

You have the following information about the movie available:

Family Zahlreich lives in a village in the mountains. They like it there because there is little traffic. It is clean and peaceful. The family has two daughters (Inge, Petra) and three sons (Heiko, Markus, Udo). They also have two cats and two dogs. Their house is large, with ten rooms. It has three bathrooms and a large cellar. It has a large garden, and a terrace but no pool. Each parent has a car but no motorcycle. The older daughter also has a car. They have a good income, because the mother is a physician. The father also has a good job.

BEISPIEL	DESIGNER	**Guten Tag! Darf ich Ihnen ein paar Fragen über** *Meine Familie* **stellen?**
	DU	**Ja, natürlich.**
	DESIGNER	**Wie heißt diese Familie?**
	DU	**Sie heißt Familie** *Zahlreich.*
	DESIGNER	**Wo wohnt diese Familie?**
	DU	**Sie wohnt....**

b. Now you are the stage designer for a movie called *Rex*, a film about the excursions of a German shepherd. In order to design an appropriate stage, you need to ask the **Regisseur** (stage director) for more information about this movie. Make sure to take notes.

You may want to ask:

What is the dog's name?
What does the dog look like?
How old is the dog?
Does this dog live with a family or in the street?
Where does the family live? In a small town? On a lake?
Does this dog have a garden? With bushes and trees?
What is this dog's favorite dish?
Does this dog have a friend with whom he likes to play?
Does the dog have a job?

Notes: _____

_____

_____

_____

_____

_____

Holt German 2 Komm mit!, Chapter 7

Name _____ Klasse _____ Datum _____

C O M M U N I C A T I V E   A C T I V I T I E S

a. You are a salesperson at a store specializing in winter clothing. A customer will come in with particular wishes. Listen carefully and respond to each request with what you have on hand from your inventory below. Make sure to use correct adjective endings! Also describe the clothes, talk about the material, and make compliments.

BEISPIEL   PARTNER **Ich hätte gern einen Gürtel.**
              DU **Wir haben lange, kurze und breite Ledergürtel.**
                  Welchen möchten Sie?
        PARTNER **Den langen Gürtel.**
              DU **Natürlich! Er passt gut zu Ihrer Hose.**

> Your store's inventory:
> **Wintermäntel — sportlich, gefüttert, geblümt**
> **Wollhemden — modisch, witzig, konservativ**
> **Blazer — grün, blau, gelb**
> **Anoraks — fesch, kariert, praktisch**
> **Hosen — weit, lässig, gestreift**

Write down what the customer wants to purchase and confirm at the end by reading the list.

BEISPIEL   **den langen Gürtel** _____   _____

_____   _____

_____   _____

b. You are preparing for a new job in Düsseldorf and want to shop for some items at a clothing store. Tell the salesperson your wishes and he or she will say what there is in stock. Remember to use correct adjective endings! Express interest and disinterest in the store's offerings, and be ready to accept compliments.

BEISPIEL   PARTNER **Guten Tag! Was möchten Sie?**
              DU **Ich hätte gern einen Faltenrock.**
        PARTNER **Gut. Wir haben sportliche, elegante und konservative**
                  Faltenröcke. Welchen möchten Sie?
              DU **Den eleganten finde ich schön.**

Clothes you would like to buy:
Anzug / Krawatte / Jacke / eine Hose / Sakko

At the end, the salesperson will recount what you would like to buy. Is this correct?

COMMUNICATIVE ACTIVITIES

 Communicative Activity 8-1 B

a. You are planning a trip to a ski resort in the Alps and want to shop for some items at a clothing store. Tell the salesperson your wishes and he or she will say what there is in stock. Remember to use correct adjective endings! Express interest and disinterest in the store's offerings, and be ready to accept compliments.

BEISPIEL PARTNER **Guten Tag! Was möchten Sie?**
                   DU **Ich hätte gern einen Gürtel.**
              PARTNER **Gut. Wir haben lange und kurze Ledergürtel.**
                       Welchen möchten Sie?
                   DU **Den langen finde ich schön.**

Clothes you would like to buy:
Mantel / Hemd / Blazer / Anorak / eine Hose

At the end, the salesperson will recount what you would like to buy. Is this correct?

b. Now you are a salesperson at a store specializing in elegant clothing. A customer will come in with particular wishes. Listen carefully and respond to each request with what you have on hand from your inventory below. Make sure to use correct adjective endings! Also describe the clothes, talk about the material, and make compliments.

BEISPIEL PARTNER **Ich hätte gern einen Faltenrock.**
                   DU **Wir haben sportliche, elegante und konservative Faltenröcke.**
                       Welchen möchten Sie?
              PARTNER **Den eleganten Rock.**
                   DU **Natürlich! Er passt gut zu Ihren Strümpfen.**

> Your store's inventory:
>   **Anzüge — sportlich, konservativ, gestreift**
>   **Krawatten — einfarbig, gepunktet, bunt**
>   **Lederjacken — weich, ärmellos, sportlich**
>   **Steghosen — braun, schwarz, rot**
>   **Sakkos — elegant, modisch, kariert**

Write down what the customer wants to purchase and confirm at the end by reading the list.

BEISPIEL   **den eleganten Rock** _____   _____

_____   _____

_____

Name _____ Klasse _____ Datum _____

a. You've risen to the top as a fashion reporter for a large agency in Hamburg. The agency has sent you to a fabulous fashion show in Munich to observe the incredibly famous pop-star Nino Angelo. So that your agency will be on top of the newest trends, you sneak off to a telephone to report back to the home office with a description of Nino's outfit. You'll have to piece back together the quick notes you took at the party, so be careful of adjective endings!

BEISPIEL   DU   **Mensch, Nino sieht einfach cool aus!**
     PARTNER   **Ja? Was trägt er?**
     DU   **Er trägt ein ganz cooles Käppi.**
     PARTNER   **Ah! Unsere Leser interessieren sich bestimmt dafür!**
                Was trägt er noch?

eine Hose — toll	und	Blouson — aus Leinen
mit		mit
Reißverschluss aus Gold		Kapuze — kariert
Knopf — sehr groß		Hemd — aus Seide, gestreift
Taschen — fetzig		
Socken — gepunktet		

b. Now you are the head of a large fashion agency in Hamburg and have sent your partner to Berlin to a fabulous fashion show where the wildly famous teen star Susi Hill is making an appearance. Your partner calls you with details about Susi's outfit so that you can get an edge in the harsh world of international (or at least German) fashion. Write down your partner's description, making sure the adjective endings are correct. Repeat your partner's description to confirm what you heard.

BEISPIEL   PARTNER   **Mensch, die Susi sieht einfach toll aus!**
           DU   **Ja? Was trägt sie denn?**
           PARTNER   **Sie trägt ein ganz schickes Käppi.**
           DU   **Toll! Unsere Leser interessieren sich dafür! Was trägt sie noch?**

_____   _____

_____   _____

_____   _____

_____   _____

_____   _____

_____   _____

_____   _____

COMMUNICATIVE ACTIVITIES

COMMUNICATIVE ACTIVITIES

 Communicative Activity 8-2 B

a. You are the head of a large fashion agency in Hamburg and have sent your partner to Munich to a fabulous fashion show where the wildly famous pop-star Nino Angelo is making an appearance. Your partner calls you with details about Nino's outfit so that you can get an edge in the harsh world of international (or at least German) fashion. Write down your partner's description, making sure the adjective endings are correct. Repeat your partner's description to confirm what you heard.

BEISPIEL PARTNER **Mensch, der Nino sieht einfach cool aus!**
     DU **Ja? Was trägt er denn?**
   PARTNER **Er trägt ein ganz cooles Käppi.**
     DU **Toll! Unsere Leser interessieren sich dafür! Was trägt er noch?**

_____ _____
_____ _____
_____ _____
_____ _____
_____ _____
_____ _____
_____ _____

b. Now you play the role of a rising fashion reporter for a large agency in Hamburg. The agency has sent you to a fabulous fashion show in Berlin to observe the incredibly famous German teen star Susi Hill. So that your agency will be on top of the newest trends, you sneak off to a telephone to report back to the home office with a description of Susi's outfit. You'll have to piece back together the quick notes you took at the party, so be careful of adjective endings!

BEISPIEL   DU **Mensch, Susi sieht einfach toll aus!**
   PARTNER **Ja? Was trägt sie?**
     DU **Sie trägt ein ganz schickes Käppi.**
   PARTNER **Ah! Unsere Leser interessieren sich bestimmt dafür!**
        Was trägt sie noch?

Minirock — abgeschnitten und Jeansweste — ärmellos
Strümpfe — gestreift   Trägerhemd — aus echter Seide
Absätze — ganz hohe   Käppi — witzig
Gürtel — geblümt
Schlaufen — sehr groß

Communicative Activity 8-3 A

a. You are the apprentice of a famous fashion designer. Today, she wants to show her new fall fashion line and asks you to announce to the audience what the models wear. Your friend has agreed to act as your prompter, giving you the names of the models and concise descriptions of their outfits. It will be up to you to market the items by giving more detailed descriptions. For example, when your friend informs you that Laura is wearing pants and a shirt, you would elaborate that she is wearing yellow silk pants and a red shirt with long sleeves, and that she looks great in that outfit. Make sure to record your announcements in order to include their description in the fashion catalogue.

BEISPIEL *Laura ist heute besonders fesch. Sie trägt eine gelbe Seidenhose und dazu ein rotes Hemd mit langen Ärmeln. Sie trägt auch ein Käppi. Diese Klamotten stehen ihr prima. Echt super.*

Name des Modells	Welche Kleider trägt sie oder er?

b. Now you will give prompts to the announcer.

Shyamali: shirt with snaps; skirt; stockings
Beverly: suit; flats
Heiko: shirt with zipper; bomber jacket; pants
Marolda: sleeveless shirt; shorts; cap
Ahmet: shirt; tie; business jacket; pants

COMMUNICATIVE ACTIVITIES

 Communicative Activity 8-3 B

a. Your friend, who is an apprentice of a famous fashion designer, has asked you to act as the prompter during a fashion show where your friend announces the models and their outfits to the audience. For every model, you'll give your friend his or her name and the clothing items he or she is wearing. Your friend will elaborate on the outfits and make them more marketable to the audience. For example, for the entry "Laura: pants; shirt" you would prompt your friend by saying, "Laura trägt eine Hose und ein Hemd."

Angelika: pants; shirt; cap
Fedwa: stirrup pants; camisole; high heels
Mark: leather jacket; boots
Vanessa: jeans vest, tie; pleated skirt
Manuela: jacket with hood

b. Now it's your turn to announce the models and their outfits to the audience. Your friend will give you prompts and you will elaborate on them to make the items more attractive to the audience. Make sure to record your announcements in order to include their description in the fashion catalogue.

Name des Modells	Welche Kleider trägt sie oder er?

Communicative Activity 9-1 A

a. You and your partner are two siblings who rarely agree on anything. The same is true for planning your upcoming vacation. Using the cues, tell your sibling the places you want to be. He or she will then suggest other places to go. At the bottom, write down the places your sibling wants to go so that you can complain to your parents.

BEISPIEL PARTNER **Hast du eine Idee?**
                    DU **Natürlich. Ich will am Strand sein.**
                PARTNER **Hm. Ich bin dafür, dass wir in die Berge fahren.**
                    DU **Ja du. Aber ich will ... sein.**

Where do you want to be? Use the correct articles and cases!

in / Boot
in / Diskothek
auf / Tennisplatz
in / Hotel

And your sibling?

Aber er/sie will ... fahren/gehen.

_____   _____

_____   _____

b. Once again, you and your partner are two siblings who rarely agree on anything. The same is still true when it comes to vacation planning. This time, using the cues, tell your sibling the places you want to go. He or she will then suggest other places he or she wants to be. At the bottom, write down the places where your sibling wants to be so that you can complain to your parents.

BEISPIEL   DU **Hast du eine Idee?**
              PARTNER **Natürlich. Ich will am Strand sein.**
                    DU **Hm. Ich schlage vor, dass wir in die Berge gehen.**
              PARTNER **Ja du. Aber ich will ... sein.**

Where do you want to go? Use the correct articles and cases!

in / Fitnessraum
in / Restaurant
auf / Berg
auf / Liegewiese

And your sibling?

Aber er/sie will ... sein.

_____   _____

_____   _____

Communicative Activity 9-1 B

a. You and your partner are two siblings who rarely agree on anything. The same is true for planning your upcoming vacation. Using the cues, tell your sibling the places you want to go. He or she will then suggest other places he or she wants to be. At the bottom, write down the places where your sibling wants to be so that you can complain to your parents.

BEISPIEL   DU **Hast du eine Idee?**
        PARTNER **Natürlich. Ich will am Strand sein.**
            DU **Hm. Ich schlage vor, dass wir in die Berge gehen.**
        PARTNER **Ja du. Aber ich will ... sein.**

Where do you want to go? Use the correct articles and cases!

in / Sauna
an / Meer
in / Fernsehraum
auf / Schiff

And your sibling?

Aber er/sie will ... sein.

_____   _____

_____   _____

b. Once again, you and your partner are two siblings who rarely agree on anything. The same is still true when it comes to vacation planning. This time, using the cues, tell your sibling the places you want to be. He or she will then suggest other places to go. At the bottom, write down the places your sibling wants to go so that you can complain to your parents.

BEISPIEL   PARTNER **Hast du eine Idee?**
            DU **Natürlich. Ich will am Strand sein.**
        PARTNER **Hm. Ich bin dafür, dass wir in die Berge fahren.**
            DU **Ja du. Aber ich will ... sein.**

Where do you want to be? Use the correct articles and cases!

in / Whirlpool
in / Hallenbad
an / See
auf / Golfplatz

And your sibling?

Aber er/sie will ... fahren/gehen.

_____   _____

_____   _____

Communicative Activity 9-2 A

a. You are a tourist in the friendly German town of Unterburg and need directions
to some famous sights in town. Ask your partner, a wizened old citizen of the
town, where the places listed below can be found. Be sure to write down the
directions so that you don't forget them.

BEISPIEL   DU **Entschuldigung! Können Sie mir bitte sagen, wo das
Rathaus ist?**
        PARTNER **Ja sicher. Das Rathaus ist gegenüber der Kirche.**
        DU **Ach, vielen Dank! Und wo ist ...?**

You want to find these places:

**Stadttor
Hauptstraße
Brunnen
Bahnhof
Kirche**

Directions: _____

_____

_____

_____

b. Now you are a venerable old citizen of another small German town: Bergheim. A
tourist comes up to you and asks directions to several well-known sights in the
town. Give the tourist directions by combining the fragments below. Be careful
with case endings!

BEISPIEL PARTNER **Entschuldigung! Können Sie mir bitte sagen, wo das
Rathaus ist?**
        DU **Ja sicher. Das Rathaus ist gegenüber der Kirche.**
        PARTNER **Ach, vielen Dank! Und wo ist ...?**

The tourist wants directions for these places:

**Krankenhaus / gegenüber / Park
Kindergarten / zwischen / Kirche, Zoo
die Fachwerkhäuser / neben / Stadion
Bücherei / durch / Park
Frisiersalon / bei / Bücherei**

Communicative Activity 9-2 B

a. You are a venerable old citizen of the small German town of Unterburg. A tourist comes up to you and asks directions to several well-known sights in the town. Give the tourist directions by combining the fragments below. Be careful with case endings!

BEISPIEL   PARTNER   **Entschuldigung! Können Sie mir bitte sagen, wo das Rathaus ist?**
                    DU   **Ja sicher. Das Rathaus ist gegenüber der Kirche.**
          PARTNER   **Ach, vielen Dank! Und wo ist ...?**

The tourist wants directions for these places:

Stadttor / neben / Brücke
Hauptstraße / durch / Stadttor
Brunnen / vor / Kirche
Bahnhof / um / Ecke
Kirche / an / Marktplatz

b. Now you are a tourist in the friendly German town of Bergheim and need directions to some famous sights in town. Ask your partner, a wizened old citizen of the town, where the places listed below can be found. Be sure to write down the directions so that you don't forget them.

BEISPIEL   DU   **Entschuldigung! Können Sie mir bitte sagen, wo das Rathaus ist?**
            PARTNER   **Ja sicher. Das Rathaus ist gegenüber der Kirche.**
                DU   **Ach, vielen Dank! Und wo ist ...?**

You want to find these places:

Krankenhaus
Kindergarten
die Fachwerkhäuser
Bücherei
Frisiersalon

Directions: _____

_____

_____

_____

Name _____ Klasse _____ Datum _____

a. Your parents want to drag you all over Europe during summer vacation, but you don't want to go trudging through one moldy old castle after another during your time off. Convince your parent that there is enough to do right in your own hometown.

BEISPIEL
DU Aber Mutti (Vati), ich will zu Hause bleiben.
MUTTI/VATI Du musst unbedingt mitfahren! In Europa gibt es viel zu tun und sehen.
DU Wir könnten auch hier ins Museum gehen.
MUTTI/VATI In Europa können wir viel mehr erfahren als hier.

What can you do in your hometown?

segeln   windsurfen   schwimmen
Tennis spielen   ins Kino gehen   tauchen

Use the lines below to write down all the things your parent says can be done in Europe.

Was kann man in Europa unternehmen?

_____

_____

_____

b. Now you are a parent who has planned a wonderful European vacation for your family. Your son or daughter, however, isn't at all thrilled, and wants to stay home and do things with his or her friends. Convince your son or daughter that he or she will actually enjoy the trip. Not only is sightseeing fun, but you have also included on your itinerary lots of other activities he or she will really enjoy.

BEISPIEL
DU Du wirst Europa gern haben. Es gibt viel zu tun.
SOHN/TOCHTER Dort gibt es nur alte Schlösser! Langweilig!
DU Nein, nein! *Schöne* Schlösser, auch heiße Diskotheken!
SOHN/TOCHTER Ich werde mich bestimmt langweilen! Aber Diskos...

What can you and your family do in Europe?

Kirchen besichtigen   Schlösser besichtigen   bergsteigen
ins Museum gehen   in Diskotheken gehen   ins Theater gehen

Use the following lines to write down what your son or daughter says you can do at home.

Was kann man in der Heimatstadt tun?

_____

_____

_____

Name _____ Klasse _____ Datum _____

Communicative Activity 9-3 B

a. You are a parent who has planned a wonderful European vacation for your family. Your son or daughter, however, isn't at all thrilled, and wants to stay home and do things with his or her friends. Convince your son or daughter that he or she will actually enjoy the trip. Not only is sightseeing fun, but you have also included on your itinerary lots of other activities he or she will really enjoy.

BEISPIEL   DU **Du wirst Europa gern haben. Es gibt viel zu tun.**
SOHN/TOCHTER **Dort gibt es nur verfallene** *(in ruins)* **Schlösser! Langweilig!**
            DU **Nein, nein!** *Schöne* **Schlösser, auch heiße Diskotheken!**
SOHN/TOCHTER **Ich werde mich bestimmt langweilen! Aber Diskos...**

What can you and your family do in Europe?

gut essen   **mit der Bahn fahren**   **Fachwerkhäuser anschauen**
windsurfen   **interessante Leute kennen lernen**   **in Parks spazieren gehen**

Use the lines below to write down all the things your son or daughter says you can do in your hometown.

Was kann man in der Heimatstadt tun?

_____

_____

_____

b. Now you are a student whose parents want to drag you all over Europe during summer vacation, but you don't want to go trudging through one moldy old castle after another during your time off. Convince your parent that there is enough to do right in your own hometown.

BEISPIEL   DU **Aber Mutti, ich will zu Hause bleiben.**
MUTTI/VATI **Du musst unbedingt mitfahren! In Europa gibt es viel zu tun und sehen.**
         DU **Wir könnten auch hier ins Museum gehen.**
MUTTI/VATI **In Europa können wir viel mehr erfahren als hier.**

What can you do in your hometown?

ins Museum gehen   **in Diskotheken gehen**   **gutes Essen**
Golf spielen   **Videos anschauen**   **Freunde besuchen**

Use the lines below to write down what your parent says you can do in Europe.

Was kann man in Europa unternehmen?

_____

_____

_____

Holt German 2 Komm mit!, Chapter 9

COMMUNICATIVE ACTIVITIES

Communicative Activity 10-1 A

a. You work for an ad agency that is trying to decide which type of television shows to sponsor for the upcoming season. You need information about the types of shows most consumers prefer. Your partner plays the roles of four different consumers. Call your partner to get the information you need.

Name	Alter	Für welche Sendungen interessieren Sie sich?	Welche Programme sehen Sie am meisten?

b. Now it's your turn to play the roles of the people listed below. Answer your partner's questions using the information given.

Name	Alter	Für welche Sendungen interessieren Sie sich?	Welche Programme sehen Sie am meisten?
Martin	18	Krimis, Western	SAT 1, RTL
Julia	31	Lustspiele, Nachrichten	ZDF, SAT 1
Jens	16	Sportsendungen, Actionfilme	ARD, RTL
Jutta	22	Lustspiele, Natursendungen	ZDF, SAT 1

Copyright © by Holt, Rinehart and Winston. All rights reserved.

COMMUNICATIVE ACTIVITIES

 Communicative Activity 10-1 B

a. Your partner needs information from the people listed in the chart below. Play the roles of these people. Your partner will call you. Share the information that your partner requests.

Name	Alter	Für welche Sendungen interessieren Sie sich?	Welche Programme sehen Sie am meisten?
Thomas	17	Abenteuerfilme, Komödien	ARD, ZDF
Sabine	33	Nachrichten, Natursendungen	SAT 1, ZDF
Jochen	14	Nachrichten, Sportsendungen	ARD, RTL
Anne	12	Natursendungen, Abenteuerfilme	ZDF, SAT 1

b. Now it's your turn to conduct the interviews. You're working for an ad agency that is attempting to decide what sorts of TV shows to sponsor for the upcoming season. You need information about the types of shows consumers prefer. Your partner will play the roles of four different consumers. Call your partner to get the information you need, and fill in the chart.

Name	Alter	Für welche Sendungen interessieren Sie sich?	Welche Programme sehen Sie am meisten?

Communicative Activity 10-2 A

a. You work for an automobile manufacturer that is attempting to develop a new line of cars. You are conducting a survey of customers to find out what features they most wish for in their cars. Ask your partner for information about the people listed in the chart. Use check marks to indicate which features they desire. When you have finished, write a short paragraph summarizing the features the customers you surveyed most wish for in a new car.

Was wünschen sie sich in einem neuen Auto?

	Stereo-radio	Automatik	Servo-lenkung	5-Gang Getriebe	Zentral-verriegelung	Alarm-anlage
Ahmet						
Katja						
Jürgen						
Thomas						
Alex						

Wofür interessieren sich die Kunden am meisten?

_____

_____

_____

_____

_____

_____

b. Now it's your turn to play the people listed below. Share the information you have with your partner.

WÜNSCHE

Kali: Servobremsen, Klimaanlage, 5-Gang Getriebe

Katrina: Alufelgen, Breitreifen, 5-Gang Getriebe

Jochen: Servobremsen, Alufelgen, 5-Gang Getriebe

Jutta: Klimaanlage, Sitzschoner, Automatik

Thorsten: Alufelgen, Breitreifen, 5-Gang Getriebe

Armin: Servobremsen, Sitzschoner, Automatik

Communicative Activity 10-2 B

a. Your partner is surveying the people listed below about what they wish for in a new car. Play the roles of the people below and share the information you have.

WÜNSCHE

Ahmet: Automatik, Stereo, Zentralverriegelung
Katja: Servolenkung, 5-Gang Getriebe, Alarmanlage
Jürgen: Stereo, 5-Gang Getriebe, Zentralverriegelung
Thomas: Stereo, Servolenkung, Alarmanlage
Alex: Servolenkung, Automatik, Alarmanlage

b. Now ask your partner for information about the people listed below. Use check marks to indicate which features they desire. When you have finished, write a short paragraph summarizing the features these customers most wish for in a new car.

Was wünschen sie sich in einem neuen Auto?

	Servo-bremsen	Klima-anlage	Sitz-schoner	Alufelgen	Breit-reifen	5-Gang Getriebe	Auto-matik
Kali							
Katrina							
Jochen							
Jutta							
Thorsten							
Armin							

Wofür interessieren sich die Kunden am meisten?

_____

_____

_____

_____

_____

_____

COMMUNICATIVE ACTIVITIES

Communicative Activity 10-3 A

a. You are one of two teenagers in a family, and you and your sibling are arguing about what to watch during prime time today. Your parents insist that you agree on what to watch before the evening line-up begins. Discuss with your partner the possibilities for the evening and tell him or her about your preferences. The two of you should come to an agreement about what to watch.

BEISPIEL   DU **Du, ich will mir unbedingt heute Abend um 18.35 „Kommissar Rex" anschauen!**

GESCHWISTER **Aber nein, das geht nicht! Zu dieser Zeit läuft im SAT 1 „Die Kids von Berlin". Das möchte ich mir anschauen!**

Welche Sendungen willst du dir anschauen?

18.05 - 18.35 / SAT 1 / Sport / „Sport Report"
18.35 - 19.25 / ZDF / Krimi / „Kommissar Rex" (ein Hund hilft der Polizei)
19.25 - 20.15 / ARD / Krimi / „Tatort"
20.15 - 21.15 / Bayern 1 / Polizei-Serie / „Alarm für Cobra 11"
21.15 - 22.15 / RTL / Action-Serie / „Einer spielt falsch"

oder

18.05 - 18.35 / ARD / lustige Videofilme / „Pleiten, Pech und Pannen"
18.35 - 19.25 / SAT 1 / Gymnasium-Serie / „Unser Lehrer Doktor Specht"
19.25 - 20.15 / RTL / Krankenhaus-Serie / „Geliebte Schwestern"
20.15 - 21.15 / RTL / Familien-Serie / „Gute Zeiten, schlechte Zeiten"
21.15 - 22.15 / Bayern 1 / Polizei-Serie / „Die Wache"

b. Use the following chart to write down the types of shows, which channels they are on, and the names of the shows your sibling says he or she wants to watch.

Welche Sendungen will er oder sie sich anschauen?

Type of Show	Channel	Name of show	Time

Upon which shows have you and your partner agreed? Write their names on the lines below.

_____

_____

COMMUNICATIVE ACTIVITIES

Communicative Activity 10-3 B

a. You are one of two teenagers in a family, and you and your sibling are arguing about what to watch during prime time today. Your parents insist that you agree on what to watch before the evening line-up begins. Discuss the possibilities for the evening with your partner and tell him or her about your preferences. The two of you should come to an agreement about what to watch.

BEISPIEL   GESCHWISTER   **Du, ich will mir unbedingt heute Abend um 18.35 „Kommissar Rex" anschauen!**

                DU   **Aber nein, das geht nicht! Zu dieser Zeit läuft im SAT 1 „Die Kids von Berlin". Das möchte ich mir anschauen!**

Welche Sendungen willst du dir anschauen?

18.05 - 18.35 / ARD / Gewinnshow / „Glücksrad"
18.35 - 19.25 / SAT 1 / Gymnasium-Serie / „Die Kids von Berlin"
19.25 - 20.15 / RTL / Arzt-Serie / „Hallo, Onkel Doktor"
20.15 - 21.15 / RTL / Familie-Serie / „Die Glückliche Familie"
21.15 - 22.15 / Bayern 1 / Krimi-Serie / „Derrick"

oder

18.05 - 18.35 / SAT 1 / Komödie-Serie / „Hör mal, wer da hämmert!"
18.35 - 19.25 / ZDF / Krimi-Polizei-Serie / „Einsatz Hamburg Süd"
19.25 - 20.15 / ARD / Krimi / „Tatort"
20.15 - 21.15 / Bayern 1 / Natursendung / „Grizzlies in Siberien"
21.15 - 22.15 / RTL / Fantasy-Serie / „Highlander"

b. Use the following chart to write down the types of shows, which channels they are on, and the names of the shows your sibling says he or she wants to watch.

Welche Sendungen will er oder sie sich anschauen?

Type of Show	Channel	Name of show	Time

Upon which shows have you and your partner agreed? Write their names on the lines below.

_____

_____

Communicative Activity 11-1 A

a. You and your partner work for a dating service that is trying to find a date for a client, Helmut. First, read through Helmut's description of his interests and his dreams for the future. Then ask your partner about his or her list of clients and fill in the chart below with the required information. Who is the best match for Helmut?

	Gewohnheiten/ Eigenschaften/Interessen	Traumpartner
Julia:		
Katja:		
Simone:		

Helmut:

Wofür ich mich am meisten interessiere, ist Reisen und die Welt sehen. Was ich mir nicht vorstellen kann, ist ein ruhiges Leben ohne Aktion. Ich bin gerne unterwegs. Zum Beispiel gehe ich vier- oder fünfmal pro Monat ins Theater. Ins Restaurant gehe ich auch ein- oder zweimal die Woche. Ich bin Vegetarier und esse kein Fleisch. Ich bin sehr aktiv and mache viele Ausflüge am Wochenende mit meinem Fahrrad. Eine Rundfahrt von 100 Kilometern ist für mich ganz normal. Mein Traum ist relativ einfach. Ich würde gern eine Partnerin finden, die auch vegetarisch isst, ein sportlicher Typ ist und sich für Reisen interessiert.

b. Now it's your turn to help your partner. Answer your partner's questions about the people listed below.

Jens: Gewohnheiten/ Eigenschaften/ Interessen: Vegetarier, politisch aktiv, umweltbewusst, Rad fahren, schwimmen, zweimal im Monat ins Theater oder in die Oper
Traumpartner: politisch aktiv, Vegetarier, kein Autofahrer

Ahmet: Gewohnheiten/ Eigenschaften/ Interessen: Sportfan, fernsehen jeden Tag (besonders Sportsendungen und Actionfilme), ein- oder zweimal im Monat ins Kino
Traumpartner: kein Vegetarier, großer Sportfan

Holger: Gewohnheiten/ Eigenschaften/ Interessen: Vegetarier, schwimmen, wandern, Rad fahren, kein Sportfan, einmal im Monat ins Konzert, Rockmusik, politisch aktiv
Traumpartner: Vegetarier, gesund, Sport treiben

COMMUNICATIVE ACTIVITIES

 Communicative Activity 11-1 B

a. You and your partner work for a dating service. Your partner has a client and needs the information you have on the clients listed below. Help your partner by answering his or her questions.

Julia: Gewohnheiten/ Eigenschaften/Interessen: Vegetarier, zweimal die Woche ins Kino, bleibt gern zu Hause, ruhiges Leben
Traumpartner: interessiert sich für sie und bleibt gern zu Hause

Katja: Gewohnheiten/ Eigenschaften/Interessen: Vegetarier, wandern, jogging, schwimmen, Kino, kein langweiliges Leben, reist gern, um die Welt reisen
Traumpartner: liebt Aktion, treibt Sport

Simone: Gewohnheiten/ Eigenschaften/Interessen: Vegetarier, Rad fahren, ab und zu zu Hause bleiben, Theater
Traumpartner: ist gern draußen aber kein Sportler, geht gern aus

b. Now it's your turn to find out who best matches your client Tara's interests. Ask your partner for the information you need to complete the chart below and decide who the best match for Tara is.

	Gewohnheiten/ Eigenschaften/Interessen	**Traumpartner**
Jens:	_____	_____
	_____	_____
	_____	_____
Ahmet:	_____	_____
	_____	_____
	_____	_____
Holger:	_____	_____
	_____	_____
	_____	_____

Tara:
Wofür ich mich interessiere ist Politik. Ich finde es sehr wichtig, dass man politisch aktiv ist. Ich bin Vegetarierin und liebe die Natur. Ich gehe am Wochenende gern wandern. Eines Tages würde ich gern auf dem Lande wohnen und ein ruhigeres Leben außerhalb der Stadt führen. Der Lärm und der Verkehr der Stadt sind mir widerlich. Ich brauche mehr Ruhe. Mein Traumpartner sollte das gleiche Ziel haben, eines Tages auf dem Lande wohnen zu wollen. Er sollte auch politisch aktiv und umweltbewusst sein. Er müsste vegetarisch essen und Sport treiben.

       Holt German 2 Komm mit!, Chapter 11

Communicative Activity 11-2 A

a. You are planning a dinner party for the people listed below. You call them on the phone to find out what they would like to eat. Your partner plays the role of the people and tells you what each would like. When you have finished, write a short paragraph describing what you will serve at your party. Base this on the chart with your guests' requests from each of the categories.

	Vorspeise	Suppe	Fisch- oder Fleischgericht	Nachspeise
Herr Maier				
Frau Kraus				
Herr Schnitt				
Frau Schnell				

Als Vorspeise _____

Als Suppe _____

Als Fischgericht _____

Als Fleischgericht _____

Als Nachspeise _____

b. Now it's your turn to help your partner. Play the roles of the people below and answer your partner's questions.

Herr Vogel: Vorspeise: gefülltes Ei **Suppe:** Gemüsesuppe **Fisch:** lieber Steinbuttfilets mit Gemüse **Fleisch:** lieber Königsberger Klopse mit Nudeln **Nachspeise:** Apfelstrudel

Frau Frank: Vorspeise: geräuchertes Forellenfilet **Suppe:** Gemüsesuppe **Fisch:** Seebarschfilet mit Pommes frites **Fleisch:** Schweinerückensteak mit Pommes frites **Nachspeise:** lieber Rote Grütze

Herr Riese: Vorspeise: gefülltes Ei **Suppe:** Nudelsuppe mit Huhn **Fisch:** lieber Seebarschfilet mit Gemüse **Fleisch:** Königsberger Klopse mit Nudeln **Nachspeise:** lieber Rote Grütze

Frau Reinecke: Vorspeise: gefülltes Ei **Suppe:** lieber Gemüsesuppe **Fisch:** Seebarschfilet auf Gemüsebett **Fleisch:** Schweinerückensteak mit Pommes frites **Nachspeise:** Rote Grütze

Communicative Activity 11-2 B

a. Your partner is planning a dinner party and is trying to decide on the menu. Play the roles of the people listed below and tell your partner what you would like to eat.

Herr Maier: Vorspeise: geräuchertes Forellenfilet **Suppe:** Gemüsesuppe **Fisch:** Seezunge mit Brokkoli **Fleisch:** Schweinerückensteak mit Pommes frites **Nachspeise:** Apfelstrudel

Frau Kraus: Vorspeise: geräuchertes Forellenfilet **Suppe:** Nudelsuppe mit Huhn **Fisch:** lieber Seezunge mit Brokkoli oder Blumenkohl **Fleisch:** Wiener Schnitzel mit Pommes frites **Nachspeise:** Rote Grütze oder Apfelstrudel

Herr Schnitt: Vorspeise: gefülltes Ei **Suppe:** Nudelsuppe mit Huhn **Fisch:** gegrilltes Seebarschfilet oder Seezunge mit Pommes frites **Fleisch:** Schweinerückensteak mit Pommes frites **Nachspeise:** lieber Apfelstrudel

Frau Schnell: Vorspeise: geräuchertes Forellenfilet **Suppe:** Gemüsesuppe **Fisch:** Seezunge mit Brokkoli **Fleisch:** Wiener Schnitzel mit Pommes frites **Nachspeise:** Rote Grütze

b. Now it's your turn to play the host. Your partner will play the roles of the people below. Call your partner and find out what he or she would like to eat. When you have finished, write a short paragraph describing what you will serve at your party, based on the information you gathered in the chart below.

	Vorspeise	**Suppe**	**Fisch- oder Fleischgericht**	**Nachspeise**
Herr Vogel	_____	_____	_____	_____
	_____	_____	_____	_____
	_____	_____	_____	_____
Frau Frank	_____	_____	_____	_____
	_____	_____	_____	_____
	_____	_____	_____	_____
Herr Riese	_____	_____	_____	_____
	_____	_____	_____	_____
	_____	_____	_____	_____
Frau Reinecke	_____	_____	_____	_____
	_____	_____	_____	_____
	_____	_____	_____	_____

Als Vorspeise _____

Als Suppe _____

Als Fischgericht _____

Als Fleischgericht _____

Als Nachspeise _____

Holt German 2 Komm mit!, Chapter 11

Communicative Activity 11-3 A

a. The German club in Berlin wants to give a dinner at a local restaurant for all its host students. You and your partner, as officers of the club, have to decide on a restaurant for the dinner. You discuss various possibilities with your partner, giving ideas about specific restaurants, the types of food each one offers, prices, and specialties. Discuss the advantages and disadvantages of each restaurant. The two of you need to agree on a restaurant for your meeting.

Was für ein Restaurant schlägst du vor?

türkisch / *Bosphoros* / Schisch-Kebab / teuer
chinesisch / *Der goldene Drache* / Huhn mit Sojasprossen / nicht teuer
italienisch / *Die Gondel* / Fettucine, Pizza / mäßig
mexikanisch / *El Sombrero* / Enchiladas, Tacos / billig

Use the following chart to fill in your partner's suggestions.

Was schlägt er oder sie vor?

Restaurant	Type	Prices	Specialties

b. The two of you have agreed on a Chinese restaurant for the German club dinner. Now you and your partner have to decide which foods to order for the buffet meal you are arranging. You discuss various possibilities with your partner, giving ideas about specific dishes and describing those dishes. Remember to use descriptive adjectives.

Welche Gerichte schlägst du vor?

sauerscharfe-Suppe / scharf, mit Gemüse
orientalischer Crevettensalat / Meeresfrüchte
Schweinefleisch mit Knoblauch / pikant
gebratener Reis (mit Gemüse) / vegetarisch
Dorschfilet mit Ingwer u. Bambus-Sprossen / gesund, mild

Use the following chart to fill in your partner's suggestions.

Was schlägt er oder sie vor?

Food	Description

Communicative Activity 11-3 B

a. The German club in Berlin wants to give a dinner at a local restaurant for all its host students. You and your partner, as officers of the club, have to decide on a restaurant for the dinner. You discuss various possibilities with your partner, giving ideas about specific restaurants, the types of food each one offers, prices, and specialties. Discuss the advantages and disadvantages of each restaurant. The two of you need to agree on a restaurant for your meeting.

Was für ein Restaurant schlägst du vor?

griechisch / *Mykonos* / Moussaka / nicht teuer
chinesisch / *Der Hunan* / süßsaures Hühnerfleisch; Reis mit Gemüse / billig
französisch / *Der Eiffelturm* / französische Zwiebelsuppe; Cordon bleu / teuer
ungarisch / *Der Zigeuner* / Gulasch / billig

Use the following chart to fill in your partner's suggestions.

Was schlägt er oder sie vor?

Restaurant	Type	Prices	Specialties

b. You have agreed on a Chinese restaurant for the German club dinner meeting. Now you and your partner have to decide which foods to order for the buffet meal you are arranging. You discuss various possibilities with your partner, giving ideas about specific dishes and describing those dishes. Remember to use descriptive adjectives.

Welche Gerichte schlägst du vor?

Reis mit Gemüse / vegetarisch
Rindfleisch mit Brokkoli / frisch, gesund, wenig Kalorien
Frühlingsrollen / knusprig, mit süßsaurer Sauce und scharfem Senf
chinesische Reispfanne mit Schweinefleisch, Rind oder Huhn / interessant
gebratene Bananen mit Vanilleeis / lecker

Use the following chart to fill in your partner's suggestions.

Was schlägt er oder sie vor?

Food	Description

Holt German 2 Komm mit!, Chapter 11

Communicative Activity 12-1 A

a. You are the customer service representative at a travel agency in Munich. A customer enters and asks you about different destinations. Offer the customer a brief description of these destinations, telling where each is and what you can do at each one. Your customer will give you feedback and make a decision about where to go.

BEISPIEL PARTNER **Ich möchte in den Urlaub fahren. Haben Sie was anzubieten?**
DU **Sicher! Hier habe ich eine Reise zu einer Oase in der Sahara. Es gibt dort auch einen Pool.**
PARTNER **Hmm. Das ist mir ein wenig zu heiß. Was haben Sie sonst noch?**

Your travel agency offers:

- **Die Küste/Griechenland:** Vergnügungsanlage „Das Rosa Schloss", Unterhaltung, Wassersport, viele junge Leute
- **Eine Insel/Sylt:** Golf, Sportanlage, feine Restaurants, Windsurfen
- **Helgoland:** Fahrrad-Depots, Tennisanlage, Angeln, Bootsfahrten, schöne Landschaft
- **Das Rote Meer/Sinai:** tauchen, bunte Fische, in der Nähe von Kairo, Pyramiden, der Nil

b. Now you are a customer interested in a nice two-week vacation. You enter a travel agency in Stuttgart to find out from the agent what vacations they offer and what one can do at the different locations. Take notes and give feedback for each destination and, at the end, decide which you want.

BEISPIEL DU **Ich möchte in den Urlaub fahren. Was haben Sie anzubieten?**
PARTNER **Also, hier habe ich eine Reise nach Istanbul in der Türkei. Es gibt dort viele Museen.**
DU **Das ist mir zu laut. Was haben Sie noch?**

Destination   **Notes**

_____   _____

_____   _____

_____   _____

_____   _____

_____   _____

COMMUNICATIVE ACTIVITIES

COMMUNICATIVE ACTIVITIES

Communicative Activity 12-1 B

a. You are a customer interested in a nice two-week vacation. You enter a travel agency in Munich to find out from the agent what vacations they offer and what one can do at the different locations. Take notes and give feedback for each destination and, at the end, decide which one you want.

BEISPIEL   DU   **Ich möchte in den Urlaub fahren. Haben Sie was anzubieten?**
PARTNER   **Sicher! Hier habe ich eine Reise zu einer Oase in der Sahara. Es gibt dort auch einen Pool.**
DU   **Das ist mir ein wenig zu heiß. Was haben Sie sonst noch?**

Destination	Notes
_____	_____
	_____
_____	_____
	_____
_____	_____
	_____
_____	_____

b. Now you are the customer service representative at a travel agency in Stuttgart. A customer enters and asks you about different destinations. Offer the customer a brief description of these destinations, telling where each is and what you can do at each one. Your customer will give you feedback and make a decision about where to go.

BEISPIEL   PARTNER   **Ich möchte in den Urlaub fahren. Haben Sie etwas anzubieten?**
DU   **Also, hier habe ich eine Reise nach Istanbul in der Türkei. Es gibt dort viele Museen.**
PARTNER   **Das ist mir zu laut. Was haben Sie noch?**

Your travel agency offers:

- **Straßburg/Frankreich:** elsässische Spezialitäten, schöne Parkanlagen, interessante Achitektur, gute Restaurants

- **Salzburg/Österreich:** Festspiele, Konzerte von Bach, Mozart und Beethoven, österreichische Backwaren, wandern in den Alpen

- **Köln/Deutschland:** Römisch-Germanisches Museum, Karneval, Wallraf-Richartz-Museum, Bootsfahrten auf dem Rhein, Ausflüge nach Bonn

- **Zermatt/die Schweiz:** am Matterhorn, Käsefondue, Schweizer Service, Ski laufen auch im Sommer, keine Autos, wandern in den Hochalpen

Communicative Activity 12-2 A

a. You own a restaurant which has a direct view of the **Kölner Dom**. A hungry traveler enters. Tell this customer about your specialties and what comes with them. The customer will record your suggestions in a travel diary. Finally, compliment your customer on the choice made.

BEISPIEL DU **Willkommen im Restaurant „Zum Domblick"! Ich sehe, Sie kommen aus Amerika. Darf ich Ihnen ein Steak mit Bohnen anbieten?**

PARTNER **Nein danke, das kann ich zu Hause essen. Was haben Sie sonst noch Gutes?**

Dishes you offer:

Hauptgerichte:	Beschreibung:
Paella, Moussaka, Tacos, Zigeunerschnitzel	Garnelen, Muscheln, Fisch, Gewürze, viel Knoblauch, reichlich Butter, Zwiebeln, importierter Teig, feinster Käse, viel Paprika, Bohnen

b. After a refreshing walk through the **Schlossgarten** in Karlsruhe you decide to have lunch. At the fringes of the **Hardtwald** you enter a restaurant called **Waldruh**. As the proprietor tells you about the menu, write the information down in your travel diary and inform the waiter of your choice.

BEISPIEL PARTNER **Willkommen im Restaurant „Waldruh"! Ich sehe, Sie kommen aus den Staaten. Möchten Sie einen Hamburger?**

DU **Aber nein! Etwas Deutsches, bitte! Was können Sie mir empfehlen?**

_____

_____

_____

_____

_____

_____

COMMUNICATIVE ACTIVITIES

 Communicative Activity 12-2 B

a. On your trip to Germany you decide to treat yourself to dinner at a restaurant in Köln. After a streetcar ride you find a nice place with view of the **Kölner Dom**. As the proprietor tells you the restaurant's specialties, you take notes of the offerings in your travel diary. Finally, make a decision on what you would like to eat and inform the proprietor of your choice.

> BEISPIEL   PARTNER **Willkommen im Restaurant „Zum Domblick"! Ich sehe, Sie kommen aus Amerika. Darf ich Ihnen ein Steak mit Bohnen anbieten?**
>
> DU **Nein danke, das kann ich zu Hause essen. Was haben Sie sonst noch Gutes?**

_____

_____

_____

_____

_____

_____

b. You operate a restaurant in Karlsruhe. An American student enters. Tell your customer about your menu (the student will write your suggestions in a diary). Finally, compliment your customer on the choice made.

> BEISPIEL   DU **Willkommen im Restaurant „Waldruh"! Ich sehe, Sie kommen aus den Staaten. Möchten Sie einen Hamburger?**
>
> PARTNER **Aber nein! Etwas Deutsches, bitte! Was können Sie mir empfehlen?**

Dishes you offer:

Hauptgerichte:	Beilagen:
Forelle, Jägerschnitzel, Wildfleischmedaillons, Schweinshaxe	mit Salzkartoffeln, mit Schnecken in Kräuterbutter, Champignons, Pommes, Sauerkraut, Bauernbrot, Torte, Eis, Kaffee, Limonade, Wasser

Holt German 2 Komm mit!, Chapter 12

Communicative Activity 12-3 A

a. You are the new owner of a small island, and intend to build a vacation resort on it. Discuss with your architect your plans for the various recreational and culinary facilities you envision having in your resort. Since there is nothing else on the island, your resort has to have all the amenities your guests could want. Be sure to include restaurants, shops of all kinds, and recreation facilities, and to explain your reasons for desiring the facilities.

Was stellen Sie sich vor?

Restaurants: Pizza Restaurant / italienisches Eiscafé / chinesisches Restaurant / Imbissstube / gutes Essen / internationale Küche
Geschäfte: Bekleidungsgeschäft / Wäscherei / Drogerie / Apotheke / Friseur
Freizeitaktivitäten: Minigolfanlage / Kraftstudio / Squashcourt / Tenniscourt / Pool / Strand

Use the following lines to write down your architect's suggestions.

Was schlägt er oder sie vor?

_____

_____

_____

_____

b. Now you are an architect whose client is building a vacation resort on an island. Find out from your client what recreational and culinary facilities he or she believes the resort should have. Give him or her suggestions for other facilities as well.

Was schlagen Sie vor?

Restaurants: Fastfood, ganz billig / französisch, zu teuer / deutsch, gutbürgerliche Küche
Geschäfte: Supermarkt / Schreibwarengeschäft
Freizeitaktivitäten: Sauna / Tischtennis / Spielplatz für Kinder / Badminton / Diskotheken / Masseur / Bücherei

Use the following lines to write down your client's ideas.

Was stellt er oder sie sich vor?

_____

_____

_____

_____

Communicative Activity 12-3 B

a. You are an architect whose client is building a vacation resort on an island. Find out from your client what recreational and culinary facilities he or she believes the resort should have. Your client seems to have forgotten about some important facilities so you give him or her some suggestions as well.

Was schlagen Sie vor?

Restaurants: mindestens vier / international / deutsch / Tanzcafé
Geschäfte: Apotheke / Lebensmittelgeschäft / Schreibwarengeschäft /
**   Spielwarengeschäft / Bekleidungsgeschäft, modische Kleidung, Badeanzüge**
Freizeitaktivitäten: Sauna / Tischtennis / Spielplatz für Kinder / Badminton

Use the following lines to write down your client's suggestions.

Was stellt er oder sie sich vor?

_____

_____

_____

_____

b. Now you are the new owner of a small island, and intend to build a vacation resort on it. Discuss with your architect your plans for the various recreational and culinary facilities you envision having in your resort. Since there is nothing else on the island, your resort has to have all the amenities your guests could want. Be sure to include restaurants, shops of all kinds, and recreational facilities, and to explain your reasons for desiring the facilities.

Was stellen Sie sich vor?

Restaurants: Meeresfrüchte Spezialitäten / genug Platz für alle Gäste
Viele kleine Geschäfte: Fahrradverleih / Bootverleih / Reisebüro
Freizeitaktivitäten: Tischtennis / Handball / Kinderpool / Pool / Strand / Tennisplatz /
Räume: Konferenzräume / Festsäle für große Gruppen und Tanzstunden

Use the following lines to write down your architect's suggestions.

Was schlägt er oder sie vor?

_____

_____

_____

_____

Wie Sie jetzt Ihren Partner finden können

Machen Sie diesen Test!

1. Interessen-Diagramm

Ihr Testergebnis und Ihre Angaben werden streng vertraulich behandelt. Kreuzen Sie an, was Sie in Ihrer Freizeit bevorzugen.

	sehr inter-essiert	gele-gent-lich	kein Inter-esse
Sport treiben	☐	☐	☐
Spaziergänge	☐	☐	☐
Fahrradfahren	☐	☐	☐
Bergwandern	☐	☐	☐
Autofahren	☐	☐	☐
Motorradfahren	☐	☐	☐
Lesen	☐	☐	☐
Musizieren	☐	☐	☐
Fernsehen	☐	☐	☐
Kino gehen	☐	☐	☐
Theater	☐	☐	☐
Oper	☐	☐	☐
Handarbeit	☐	☐	☐
Basteln	☐	☐	☐
Gartenarbeit	☐	☐	☐
Parties	☐	☐	☐
Diskussionen	☐	☐	☐
Einkaufen	☐	☐	☐
Stadtbummel	☐	☐	☐
Freunde treffen	☐	☐	☐
Familienfeiern	☐	☐	☐
Hausarbeit	☐	☐	☐
Kochen	☐	☐	☐
Sonstiges	☐	☐	☐

3. Partnerprofil

Wählen Sie aus diesen Eigenschaften 5 aus, die Sie von Ihrem Partner erwarten:

☐ häuslich   ☐ ehrlich
☐ natürlich   ☐ zärtlich
☐ treu   ☐ tolerant
☐ modisch   ☐ sportlich
☐ sparsam   ☐ kinderlieb

Wünsche zum Partner/in:

Alter: von _____ bis _____ Jahre

Größe: von _____ bis _____ cm

Reißen oder schneiden Sie einfach diese ganze Seite heraus und senden Sie diese heute noch in einem unfrankierten Briefumschlag ab an:
    VIP Winterhuder Weg 62,
    22085 Hamburg

2. Angaben zu Ihrer Person Bitte in Blockschrift   FE 837

Herr ☐   Frau ☐   Fräulein ☐

Name: _____

Vorname: _____

Str. Nr. _____

PLZ/Ort: _____

Vorw.
Telef. _____ Geb.Dat: _____

Staatsangehörigk. _____ Körpergr: _____ cm

REALIA

Kleinanzeigen Bestellschein
von privat an privat

in über
150.000
Zeitungen

Bitte ausgefüllten Coupon ausschneiden und senden an das Hagener Tagesblatt, Meierstraße 5, 63570 Hagen

REALIA

Samstag **Mittwoch** Flohmarkt/ Personalanzeigen	**Donnerstag** **Mittwoch** Kreisanzeiger Einkauf-Tip
Gewünschtes bitte ankreuzen	Gewünschtes bitte ankreuzen
bis 4 Zeilen = € 8,- ☐	Bis 4 Zeilen = € 10,- ☐
5 Zeilen = € 9,- ☐	5 Zeilen = € 11,- ☐
6 Zeilen = € 10,- ☐	6 Zeilen = € 12,- ☐
7 Zeilen = € 11,- ☐	7 Zeilen = € 13,- ☐
8 Zeilen = € 12,- ☐	8 Zeilen = € 14,- ☐

Nur bei Chiffreanzeigen.

☐ **Ich hole die Zuschriften ab.** (+ € 1,50)
☐ **Ich bitte um Zusendung der Zuschriften.** (+ € 4,50)

Name _____

Straße _____ Wohnort (____) _____

Scheck über € _____ liegt bei. _____

Buchen Sie € _____ von Konto-Nr. _____ ab.

Bank _____

Bankleitzahl _____

Unterschrift _____

Hagener Tagesblatt
Meierstraße 5.
63570 Hagen

Telefon: 0605/814-220-211, Fax: 06012/12387

Realia 1-1: Steckbrief form

1. **Writing** Have students fill out the form. Remind students how Germans write the date on official forms. For example, June 8, 1980 would be written 8.6.80. Explain any unfamiliar vocabulary.

2. **Speaking** Have students pair up; one person is an interviewer, and the other is the interviewee. The interviewer fills out the form by asking the other person for the pertinent information.

3. **Speaking** Have students conduct a survey of the class to find out how many students share the same interests.

Realia 1-2: Personality profile for a dating service

1. **Writing** Ask students for what they think the form is used. Have them guess the meaning of unfamiliar words or terminology. Explain any unfamiliar vocabulary or abbreviations. Then have students fill out the form with all the pertinent information.
   Testergebnis: *test result*   **Angabe:** *information*
   streng vertraulich behandelt: *handled strictly confidentially*
   bevorzugen: *favor*
   unfrankierten Briefumschlag: *postage due envelope*

2. **Speaking** Have students pair up; one person works for the dating service and the other is a customer. The person working for the dating service asks the other student for the pertinent information.

3. **Speaking** Conduct a class survey, asking questions such as: **Wie viele interessieren sich für ...? Seid ihr sehr interessiert, gelegentlich, oder habt ihr kein Interesse? Welche Eigenschaften sind euch wichtig? Häuslich? Natürlich? Treu?**

Realia 1-3: Newspaper advertisement form

1. **Speaking** Ask students for what they think this form is used. Then have them try to guess the meaning of unfamiliar words or abbreviations. When they have finished, explain any unfamiliar terminology or abbreviations.
   Chiffreanzeigen: *coded ads*   **ankreuzen:** *to check off*
   Zusendung: *delivery*   **Zeilen:** *lines*
   Zuschriften: *letter/official communication (in this case the ad)*
   Buchen: *to debit one's account*
   Konto-Nr: *account number*
   Bankleitzahl: *routing number for the bank*

2. **Writing** Have students write their own personal ad and fill out the form.

3. **Speaking** Have students share their personal ad with the class.

4. **Pair work** Have students work in pairs to develop a personal ad. One person works for the newspaper, and the other is placing the ad. The person at the newspaper will ask questions to get the entire form filled out, including personal, price, and payment information.

Realia 2-1

REALIA

Meine Wochenpläne für _____

Name: _____

Zeit	Mo	Di	Mi	Do	Fr	Sa	So

Qualität und Frische | WERT MARKT | dauernd echt billig

Aus unserer Metzgerei und Fischabteilung!

Hähnchenkeulen
Hkl. A, gefroren
1-kg-Btl. **1.98**

Schweine-Schnitzel
zart und saftig
1 kg **4.48**

Forellen Lebendgewicht
kein Schlachtaufpreis
1 kg **4.80**

Steak
aus dem Schäufele
geschnitten   1 kg **2.98**

Rinder-Lende
(Roastbeef), zart
abgehangen 1 kg **7.98**

Puten-Unterkeulen
frisch. Hkl. A
1 kg **1.33**

Aus unserer Obst- und Gemüseabteilung!

1 kg Bananen
besonders schön   **-.48**

500 g frischer Spargel
aus Griechenland Kl. I,
16 mm   Bund **1.98**

2,5 kg Speise-Frühkartoffeln
Kl. I vorw. fest
kochend   Btl. **0.98**

Frisch aus der Brot- u. Backwarentheke!

Bauernbrot
Roggenmischbrot
mit Natursauerteig
1000 g-Laib   **1.59**

Bäcker-Kreppel
mit feiner Fruchtfüllung
Stück **0.50**

4-Korn-Brötchen
ballaststoffreiches
Mehrkornbrötchen
Stück **0.45**

Aus unserer Käsetheke!

Holl. Gouda oder -Edamer
Schnittkäse 48% Fett i. Tr.
frisch vom Laib,
am Stück   100 g **0.49**

Käse-Aufschnitt
Naturkäsescheiben
40/45% Fett i. Tr.
250-g-Packung   **1.79**

Camembert
Weichkäse
30% Fett i. Tr.
200-g-Packung   **1.19**

Solange Vorrat reicht!   Öffnungszeiten: **Irrtum vorbehalten!**
Montag- Freitag   6.00 - 20.00 Uhr   Samstag   8.00 - 16.00 Uhr

REALIA

Realia 2-3

Mit dem BücherScheck treffen Sie jeden Geschmack.

Der eine liebt Gartenkunst, der andere bildende Kunst. Aber wer liebt was? Und wer liebt welche Bücher ganz besonders? Mit einem BücherScheck als Geschenk liegen Sie richtig. Der Beschenkte hat die freie Auswahl im Buchhandel, denn da löst er seinen Scheck gegen sein Wunschbuch ein. Und freut sich, daß man mit einem BücherScheck seinen Geschmack getroffen hat. **BücherSchecks gibt es von €5 bis €100 bei Ihrem Buchhändler.**

Buchhandlung am Markt
Neumarkt 11
6700 Neustadt

BücherScheck

00091254438   006237408

REALIA

Realia 2-1: Weekly calendar

1. **Speaking** Review time-telling and days of the week.

2. **Writing** Have students fill out the calendar with their plans for the week. Then tell students to exchange papers with each other. Have each student write a paragraph describing what the other person has planned for the week.

3. **Speaking** Have students pair up. Their schedules should be blank. Have them interview each other about what the other has planned for the week and fill out the calendar. When they have finished, they should share the information they collected about the other person with the rest of the class.

Realia 2-2: Grocery store ad

1. **Speaking** Have students scan the ad for familiar words and cognates. Explain any unfamiliar words.
   Schäufele *shoulder cut*
   abgehangen *aged*
   Forellen *trout*
   kein Schlachtaufpreis *no butchering surcharge*
   Unterkeulen *legs*
   ballaststoffreich *rich in fiber*
   Roggenmischbrot *mixed rye and wheat bread*
   Mehrkornbrötchen *multi-grain rolls*
   Natursauerteig *naturally leavened (sour) dough*

2. **Writing** Have students plan a meal based on the items from the ad.

3. **Speaking** Have students role-play conversations they would have in the different departments of the store. They should discuss food items, quantities, and prices.

Realia 2-3: Gift certificate ad

1. **Speaking** Have students scan the ad for familiar words and cognates. Explain any unfamiliar words.
   die Kunst *art*
   der Beschenkte *receiver of the gift*
   die Auswahl *choice*
   der Geschmack *taste*

2. **Writing** Have students make a list of family members or friends and the type of books each would like to receive as a gift.

3. **Speaking** Have students help you make "**BücherSchecks**" in various amounts and distribute them around the class. Have students work in pairs; one plays the customer buying a book with a "**BücherScheck**" and the other plays the salesperson.

Realia 3-1

Ingolstadt im Herzen Bayerns
bietet viele Möglichkeiten
für Altstadtbummel, Wandern,
Radwandern, Museen,
Kunst, Baden und Sport.
Vor allem aber: ein starkes Stück
Altbayern und Tradition.

Bitte schicken Sie mir kostenlos Informationsmaterial.

_____

Name

_____

Straße

_____

Wohnort

Fremdenverkehrsamt, Rathausplatz 4, 85049 Ingolstadt
Tel 0841/305-1098, Fax. 0841/305-1099

Advertisement, "Ingolstadt," from *Bunte*. Reprinted by permission of **Städt. Fremdenverkehrsamt**, Ingolstadt.

REALIA

Name _____ Klasse _____ Datum _____

GEHEIMTIPS AUS LEIPZIG

ÜBERNACHTEN: Jugendherberge Leipzig, Käthe-Kollwitz-Str. 62-66, Tel.: 0341/470530; Jugendherberge am Auensee, Gustav-Esche-Str. 4, Tel.: 0341/57189; Zimmervermittlung über das Fremdenverkehrsamt Leipzig, Tel.: 0341/7959308

ESSEN: Restaurant „Mövenpick", Am Naschmarkt; McDonalds in der Fußgängerzone; El Greco, Delitzscher Landstr. 56

AUSGEHEN: Biker-Treff „Chopper" (schräger Laden mit alten Motorrädern eingerichtet), Weißenfelserstr. 63, (Saft, Cola, Wasser 1 €); Moritz-bastei, Universitätsstr. 9, (Cola 1 €, Kaffee 0,75 €, Käsebrötli 0,75 €, Apfel 30 Cent), Kabarett Pfeffer-mühle, Thomaskirchhof 16, Tel.: 0341/295877

DISCO: Disco in der Moritzbastei, Universitätsstr. 9, (Mi., Fr., Sa., open end, Eintritt 2 €), Disco im Haus „Am Auensee", Gustav-Esche-Str. 4, (im Sommer jedes Wochenende) gleich neben dem Zeltplatz, s.a. Übernach-tung)

SIGHTSEEING: Tolle historische Einkaufspassagen aus der Vorkriegszeit. Unbedingt sehen: Die Mädler-Passage (wird gerade frisch renoviert); Altes Rathaus mit Stadtgeschichte-Museum, Neues Rathaus, Thomaskirche, Nicolaikirche

SHOPPING: Fußgängerzone mit vielen kleinen Jeans-Boutiquen und dem täglichen Markt; Mädler-Passage; der absolute In-Laden „Collins", Jahn-Allee/Ecke Thomasiusstraße

BADEN: Auensee (s. Adresse „Haus Auensee"), Kulkwitzer See (mit der Straßenbahn vom Hauptbahnhof in 45 Minuten zu erreichen)

SCHLECHT-WETTER-TIPS: Filmbühne Capitol, Petersstraße; Filmclub Titanic (Programmkino), Katharinenstr; UCI Kinowelt (10 Cinemas), Merseburger Str. 17a, 0-4201 Günthersdorf (15 Min. v. Leipzig-City); Grassimuseum Leipzig mit Museum des Kunsthandwerks, Musikinstrumente-Museum der Universität Leipzig; Museum der Bildenden Künste, Dimitroff-Platz 1

REALIA

"Geheimtips aus Leipzig" from *Mädchen*. Reprinted by permission of **MVG Medien Verlagsgesellschaft mbH & Co.**

Realia 3-3

Explanation of abbreviations:
3 Ü = three nights **F** = breakfast included **DZ** = room with two beds **DU** = shower **WC** = toilet
Vollpension = three meals included **Halbpension** = breakfast and either lunch or dinner included

Aus Freude am Reisen

Werfenweng im Salzburger Land
Alpin – Langlauf – Wandern
4 Tage vom 14.1. abends – 18. 1. 94
***Hotel 3 UF/DZ/DU/WC....................169,–€

Schneewochenende im Ahrntal (Südtirol)
4 Tage vom 26. 1. abends – 30. 1. 94
***Hotel 3 Ü/Halbpension DZ/DU/WC.............169,–€

Karneval in Nizza
Italienische Palmenriviera
4 Tage vom 17. 2. abends – 21. 2. 94
***Hotel 3 Ü/Vollpension DZ/DU/WC.................184,–€
U/F 199,–€

„Biersause" in Prag
3 Tage vom 4. 3. –6. 3. 94
***Hotel, 2 ÜF/DZ/DU/WC
Essen – Bierprobe – Musik –
fachkundige Führung Prag – Karlsbad..................177,–€

Frühling in der Toscana
Florenz – Siena
4 Tage vom 18. 3. abends – 22. 3. 94
***Kur-Hotel, 3 Ü/Halbpension DZ/DU/WC ....179,–€

Ostern in die südliche Sonne
Mallorca, Bus–Schiffs–Reise
10 Tage vom 26. 3.– 4. 4. 94
***Hotel, DZ/DU/WC/Balkon
7 Übern, Frühstücks u. Abend–Buffet.....................443,–€

Ungarische Städte und Puszta–Romantik
Budapest – Eger
5 Tage vom 5. 4. abends – 10. 4. 94.
4/U/Halbp.im Komfort–Hotel Budapest.....................234,–€

Traumziel: Italienische Palmenriviera
Gelegenheit: Monaco – Nizza
4 Tage 6. 4. abends – 10. 4. 94
***Hotel, DZ/DU/WC, 3 Ü/Vollpension ....199,–€
U/F 159,–€

Ostseeküste mit Insel Rügen
4 Tage vom 14. 4. – 17. 4. 94
3 Ü/F, Hotel DZ/DU/WC...............................184,–€

Paris
3 Tage vom 14. 4. abends – 17. 4. 94
2 Ü/F, Hotel DZ/DU/WC................................199,–€

Große Pilger–Reise
Lourdes – Santiago de Compostela – Fatima
14 Tage vom 6. 5. – 19. 5. 94
13 Ü/Halbp, gute** und ***Hotels...................824,–€

Spreewald – Sächsische Schweiz
Dresden – Meißen
4 Tage vom 26. 5. –29. 5. 94
3 Ü/F, Hotel DZ/DU/WC................................159,–€

Berlin – Spreewald
4 Tage vom 16. 6. – 19. 6. 94
3 Ü/F, Hotel, DZ/DU/WC................................278,–€

London
3 Tage vom 28. 7. abends – 31. 7. 94
U/F, London, eine Schiffsübernachtung..................209,–€

Schlesien – Riesengebirge
Breslau – Hirschberg – Schweidnitz–
Krummhübel – Schneekoppe – Waldenburg
6 Tage vom 2. 8 – 7. 8. 94
5 Ü/Halbpension, ***Hotel DZ/DU/WC..............293,–€

Lüneburger Heide – Hamburg
3 Tage vom 12. 8. – 14. 8. 94
2 Ü/F Hotel DZ/DU/WC................................134,–€

Schottland – Bus-Schiffs-Reise
Zu den Highlands und Orkney–Inseln
10 Tage vom 27. 8.–5. 9. 94
7 Ü/Halbpension, gute Hotels DZ/DU/WC
2 Schiffsübernachtungen..............................798,–€

Traumziel: Italienische Palmenriviera
Gelegenheit: Monaco – Nizza
4 Tage vom 14. 9. abends – 18. 9. 94
3 Ü/Vollpension ***Hotel DZ/DU/WC.................199,–€
Ü/F 159,–€

Erstklassiges Mähren
Super Komfort in Brünn
4 Tage vom 15. 9.– 18. 9. 94. 3 Ü/Halbpension***Hotel
Alle Ausflugst, 1 Bier– und 1 Weinabend................198,–€

Sizilien – Malta
Bus–Schiffs–Reise
12 Tage vom 28. 9. –9. 10. 94
10 Ü/Halbpension, gute Hotels, DZ/DU/WC
1 Schiftsübernachtung................................792,–€

Ungarn
Weinlese am Plattensee
Budapest – Puszta–Programm
5 Tage 14. 10. abends – 19. 10. 94
4 Ü/Halbpension, Kurhotel, DZ/DU/WC..............299,–€

Rom – Florenz
Gelegenheit Insel Capri
6 Tage vom 31. 10. abends –6. 11. 94
4 Ü/V, ***Hotel Rom, 1 Ü/F, ***Hotel Florenz
Papstaudienz.............Ü/F 298,–€
HP 299,–€

Mallorca in südlicher Sonne
Bus–Schiffs–Reise
9 Tage vom 12. 11. –20. 11. 94. ***Hotel DZ/DU/WC/Balkon
6 Ü/Frühstücks– und Abend–Buffet..................413,–€

Hamburg – Ostsee – Dänemark
2 Tage vom 26. 11. –27. 11. 94
1 Ü/F, Hotel, DZ/DU/WC................................74,–€

Weihnachtsmarkt in Dresden
Holzspielwaren im Erzgebirge
2 Tage vom 3. –4. 12. 94
1 Ü/F, Hotel DZ/DU/WC................................74,–€

„Das Besondere" Große Skandinavienreise
Auf den schönsten Wegen zum Nordkap Bus–Schiffs–Reise
15 Tage vom 25.6. –9. 7. 94
Kopenhagen – Oslo – Helsinki – Stockholm – Lofoten – 2 Etappen mit dem Postschiff 12 Ü/Halbpension *** und *** Hotels, 2.
Schiffsübern/DU/WC/Frühst–Buffet.......................1.399,–€

Geringe Änderungen behalten wir uns vor

Alle Fahrten mit modernsten Fernreisebussen und Bordservice
Vereine und Gesellschaften erhalten ein spezielles Angebot. Bitte fordern Sie unser ausführliches Programm an!

Hedrich-Reisen

63584 Gründau – Gewerbestraße 1
Telefon 0 60 58/28 24 – Fax 0 60 58/14 50

Realia 3-1: Ingolstadt ad

1. **Speaking** Ask students what they think the ad is for. What types of activities are mentioned in the ad? Would they be interested in finding out more about Ingolstadt?

2. **Writing** Have students write their own ads promoting the city/town in which they live, or a place they recently visited.

3. **Speaking** Have students pair up and act out the following situation. One works at a tourist information desk and the other is a tourist inquiring about what there is to do in their city. This could also be done as a phone call.

Realia 3-2: Tips for Leipzig

1. **Speaking** Have students scan the article for familiar words and cognates. Ask students: Do the pictures tell you what each paragraph is about? Explain any unfamiliar words.

2. **Writing** Divide the class into eight groups, one for each category: **Übernachten, Essen, Ausgehen, Disco, Sightseeing, Shopping, Baden und Schlecht-Wetter-Tips.** Have the groups write an insider's tip list about the city/town in which they live for their respective categories. When they have finished, have them share their lists with the class.

3. **Writing** Have each student write a description of a city/place they recently visited. Using the eight categories, have them describe where they stayed, where they ate, where they went, etc.

Realia 3-3: Travel ad

1. **Speaking** Ask students what they think the ad is for. Have them scan for familiar words and cognates. Explain unfamiliar words and abbreviations. Ask questions about the ad: **Was ist teurer: Halbpension oder Übernachtung mit Frühstück?**

2. **Speaking** Have students pair up and role-play the following situation. One of them is the customer asking about special trips and hotel accommodations/cost and the other is the travel agent.

3. **Writing** Have students either individually or in groups write a travel ad that would provide a German-speaking tourist with similar information about places in the United States.

Realia 4-1

REALIA

Steppen Sie sich fit!

Ideal für

- **Herz/Kreis-lauf**
- **zur Figur-formung**
- **zum Abneh-men**

Bekannt aus der TV-Werbung

Mini-Stepper

Der Mini-Stepper bringt ihren Kreislauf in Schwung, stärkt Herz und Muskulatur und verbessert Durchblutung und Ve-nentätigkeit. Sie trainieren ganz einfach wetterunabhängig in Ihrem Zimmer. Der Mini-Stepper braucht nur wenig Platz (Größe 35 x 37 x 19cm). Der hydrauli-sche Tretmechanismus ist in der Tritt-höhe verstellbar und für jedes Familien-mitglied individuell anzupassen. So hält sich die ganze Familie fit. Schon nach wenigen Wochen Training mit dem Mini-Stepper werden Sie bemerken, wie durchtrainiert Ihr Körper und wie straffer und schlanker Ihre Figur wird. Testen Sie den aus der TV-Werbung bekannten Mini-Stepper. TÜV/GS-geprüft.

nur EUR 49.⁹⁰

Bestell-Coupon

☐ **Ja**, schicken Sie mir

_____ Stück Mini-Stepper (Best.-Nr. 5901-4)

Vorname _____ Name _____

Straße _____ Nr. _____

Plz _____ Ort _____

Ich zahle

☐ mit beiliegendem Verrechnungsscheck (zzgl. 5.95 für Porto und Verpackung)

☐ per Nachnahme (zzgl. DM 8.50 Nachnahmegebühren)

Datum _____ Unterschrift _____ NG

Gleich einsenden an:

CONTERNA-VERSAND GmbH
Gutenbergstr.2 · 75206 Keltern
Tel. 07236/361 · Fax. 07236/7480

Advertisement, "Steppen Sie sich fit!," from *Neue Gesundheit*. Reprinted by permission of **Conterna-Versand GmbH.**

Fitness über alle Distanzen

Brot und Butter sind eine ideale Kombination. Das besonders leicht verdauliche Milchfett der Butter und die Kohlenhydrate des Brotes bringen Leistung und Energie. Zusätzlich versorgt uns Brot mit wichtigen Ballaststoffen.

Ein Stück Käse verwöhnt jeden Gaumen und versorgt uns mit Eiweiß und dem gut bekömmlichen Milchfett.

Milch enthält wertvolles Milcheiweiß und Milchzucker für mehr Vitalität und ist unser wichtigster Calcium-Lieferant.

Mit dem Tag Schritt halten. Dafür gibt es ein gutes Rezept: Bewegung und eine gesunde, ausgewogene Ernährung mit Nahrungsmitteln aus Deutschland. Sie enthalten Eiweiß, Kohlenhydrate, Fett, Vitamine und Mineralstoffe und sind die idealen Fitmacher: unübertroffen in Frische, Qualität und Vielfalt. Für mehr Geschmack am gesunden Leben.

Excerpt from advertisement, "Fitness über alle Distanzen," from *Freundin*. Reprinted by permission of **FCB Hamburg/CMA 53177 Bonn, Germany**.

R E A L I A

Realia 4-3

VITAMINE

Was ist worin ent-halten?

Vitamin		Vitaminquelle
A	(Retinol)	Kalbsleber, Feldsalat, Spinat, Grünkohl
D	(Calciferol)	Hering, Lachs, Aal
E	(Tocopherol)	Weizenkeimöl, Sonnenblumenöl, Grünkohl, Erbsen
K		Tomaten, Kopfsalat, Leber, grünes Gemüse
B$_1$	(Thiamin)	Schweinefleisch, Vollkornbrot, Kartoffeln
B$_2$	(Riboflavin)	Trinkmilch, Buttermilch, Schweine- und Rinderleber
B$_6$	(Pyridoxin)	Sardinen, Makrelen, Kotelett, Bananen
B$_{12}$	(Cobalamin)	Kalbsleber, Trinkmilch, Speisequark
Biotin		Trinkmilch, Leber, Sojabohnen
Folsäure		Leber, Tomaten (roh), Blumenkohl, Weißkohl (roh), Wirsingkohl
Niacin		Erbsen, Rind- und Schweinefleisch (ohne Fett), Brathuhn, Sardinen
Pantothensäure		Ostseehering, Leber, Steinpilze, Erbsen, Wassermelone
C	(Ascorbinsäure)	Schwarze Johannisbeeren, Paprika (roh), Weißkohl (roh), Kiwi, Orange, Erdbeeren

Adaptation of chart, "Vitamine: Was ist worin enthalten?," from *Neue Apotheken Illustrierte Extra*, p. 16.
Reprinted by permission of ***Govi-Verlag***.

Realia 4-1: Mini-stepper ad

1. **Speaking/Reading** Have students scan the ad for cognates and familiar words. Explain any unfamiliar words. Ask students what sort of claims the ad is making about the product. What are its positive features?

Kreislauf *blood circulation*	**abnehmen** *losing weight*
Durchblutung *blood supply*	**Venentätigkeit** *vein capacity/action*
straffer *tauter/tighter*	**wetterunabhängig** *not dependent on the weather*

2. **Speaking** Have students role-play commercials for the product. Two students could play a reporter interviewing a satisfied customer about the health benefits of the **Mini-Stepper**.

3. **Writing** Have students write a paragraph describing the benefits of the **Mini-Stepper**.

4. **Group Work** Have students combine their efforts from #2 and #3 and prepare a TV commercial for exercise equipment.

Realia 4-2: Nutritional ad

1. **Speaking/Reading** Read the advertisement to the students and explain any unfamiliar items:

Gaumen *palate; taste buds*	**Eiweiß** *protein, also egg white*
Milchfett *fat content of milk*	**Kohlenhydrate** *carbohydrates*
Ballaststoffe *fiber*	**Milcheiweiß** *milk protein*
Calcium-Lieferant *source of calcium*	

   Ask students what the objective of the advertisment is. What do butter, milk, and cheese have in common? (They are all derived from milk.) What does this ad attempt to do? (educate people on the benefits of products derived from milk, sell milk)

2. **Speaking** Have students describe what they eat and for what reason. For example: **Ich trinke viel Milch, weil sie für meine Gesundheit gut ist.** Alternatively, ask them to tell you what they eat for breakfast, lunch, and supper. For example, **Zum Frühstück esse ich ...**

3. **Writing** Have students write an ad promoting their favorite foods.

Realia 4-3: Vitamin chart

1. **Reading/Writing** Have students read through the list **Vitaminquelle** and explain the new vocabulary as you go along.

Kalbsleber *calf liver*	**Grünkohl** *kale*
Lachs *salmon*	**Aal** *eel*
Sonnenblumenöl *sunflower oil*	**Weizenkeimöl** *oil pressed from wheat seeds*
Kotelett *pork chop*	**Blumenkohl** *cauliflower*
Weißkohl *white cabbage*	**Steinpilze** *edible mushrooms*
Erdbeeren *strawberries*	**schwarze Johannisbeeren** *black currants*

2. **Listening** Make statements about different items on the list and have students tell you if your statements are true or false. For example, you might say **Durch Kalbsleber bekommt man Vitamin D. (stimmt nicht; durch Hering, Lachs und Aal bekommt man Vitamin D.)**

3. **Speaking** Have students describe in German what they had to eat recently and what vitamins their food contained. What are some other sources of vitamins?

4. **Writing** Have students write a paragraph on what items from the list they would or would not like to eat and why or why not.

Realia 5-1

Advertisement, "Joghurt," from *Mädchen*. Reprinted by permission of **Centrale Marketing Gesellschaft der deutschen Agrarwirtschaft mbH**.

»Mir zuliebe. Landliebe.«

Ob nun unser **Fruchtjoghurt** das Feinste ist, was einem Dessertlöffel passieren kann, oder ob dies doch eher für unseren **Früchtequark** gilt, darüber streiten die Genießer.

Wobei wiederum die schönste Einigkeit herrscht, daß die rahmig-frische **Landmilch**, aus der wir diese Leckereien machen, auch pur getrunken ein Hochgenuß ist.

Advertisement, "Mir zuliebe. Landliebe.," from *TV*. Reprinted by permission of **Südmilch AG**.

REALIA

Realia 5-3

Essen Sie gesund?

Kreuzen Sie bei den folgenden Fragen die für Sie zutreffende Antwort an:

③ Was naschen Sie abends beim Fernsehen?

A Am liebsten Pralinen oder ein Stück Schokolade. ☐

B Ungesalzene Erdnüsse, aber nicht zu viele. ☐

C Ich esse einen Apfel oder eine Banane. ☐

① Welches Brot essen Sie am liebsten?

A Französisches Weißbrot. ☐

B Normales Mischbrot. ☐

C Vollkornbrot. ☐

Die Ergebnisse:

Am häufigsten C:
Ihre Eßgewohnheiten sind äußerst gesund. Gönnen Sie sich doch einmal einen kleinen Ausrutscher.

Am häufigsten B:
Ihre Eßgewohnheiten sind ausgewogen. Wenn Sie einmal über die Stränge schlagen, dann gleichen Sie das wieder aus.

Am häufigsten A:
Sie müssen Ihre Eßgewohnheiten ändern. Ihrem Essen fehlen Vitamine und Ballaststoffe. Unser Tip an Sie: Nehmen Sie NatuVit. Es mindert das Hungergefühl, regt die Verdauung an und unterstützt die Diät. Der Mangel an Ballaststoffen wird durch die regelmäßige Einnahme ausgeglichen.

② Wenn's mittags schnell gehen muß, was essen Sie?

A Am liebsten Bratwurst mit Pommes. ☐

B Einen Joghurt mit Früchten. ☐

C Einen gemischten Salat mit Joghurt-Dressing. ☐

Excerpt from advertisement, "Essen Sie gesund?," from *Neue Apotheken Illustrierte Extra*, p. 17. Reprinted by permission of **Asta Medica AG**.

REALIA

Realia 5-1: Joghurt ad

1. **Listening** Make statements about the ad and have students say whether your statements are true or false.

2. **Reading** Have students read the text in the ad and then answer questions such as **Warum mag die Frau Joghurt? Wie überrascht sie ihre Freunde? Was kann man für „1 € in Briefmarken" bestellen?**

3. **Speaking** Have students tell you everything they see in the picture. Have them imagine what this woman is probably like and describe her, both the way she looks and the kind of personality they think she has, based on the text.

4. **Speaking/Group Work** Have students work in small groups to invent conversations that might take place between this woman and her friends when she serves them dinner. They should include comments about what she is serving and her attitude toward **Joghurt**.

Realia 5-2: Ad for Quark and Joghurt

1. **Vocabulary Practice** Have students identify any cognates that might help them better understand the text. Have them identify the superlative forms (**das Feinste, die schönste ...**). Can they tell you why one of these words is used with "**das**" and the other with "**die**"?

2. **Reading** Have students read through the text and then answer questions such as **Wer sind „die Genießer"? Worüber streiten sich die Genießer?**

3. **Listening** Make statements about the text and have students either answer multiple choice questions or say whether your statements are true or false.

4. **Speaking** Have students describe the picture, telling what they see in the foreground (**Vordergrund**) and in the background (**Hintergrund**). Are they able to discern anything about the relationship between the background and the foreground? (cows, farm, nature = natural products)

Realia 5-3: Nutrition test

1. **Reading** Have students take the test and discern the category of eaters to which they belong.

2. **Listening** Describe the foods/types of food eaten by people in these groups and have students determine which group you are describing.

3. **Reading/Writing/Pair Work** Have pairs of students figure out what **NatuVit** is. Have them write out the definition and describe what the product does.

4. **Group Work** Have small groups of students write and perform for the class a TV commercial for **NatuVit**.

REALIA

Mehr drin ★ mehr dran!

topfitz ®
MultiVitamin+Mineral

Vitamin C
Vitamin E
Vitamin B_1
Vitamin B_2
Vitamin B_6
Vitamin B_{12}
Calciumpantothenat
Nicotinamid
Folsäure
Biotin
Calcium
Kalium
Magnesium

★ **Alles in einer Brausetablette!**
Nicht nur Vitamine, sondern auch Mineralstoffe.

Hervorragender Geschmack, ausgewogene Dosierung, schnelle Aufnahme.

HERMES – Qualität aus Ihrer Apotheke!

HERMES ARZNEIMITTEL GMBH, Pharma · Ernährung · Kosmetik, 82049 Großhesselohe/ München

Advertisement, "Mehr drin * mehr dran!: topfitz® MultiVitamin+Mineral," from *FUNK UHR*. Reprinted by permission of *Hermes Arzneimittel GmbH*.

Excerpt from advertisement, "EUBOS® Sonnenschutz," from *petra*. Reprinted by permission of *Dr. Hobein & Co. Nachf. GmbH*.

Name _____ Klasse _____ Datum _____

Realia 6-3

REALIA

Advertisement, "Kuren in besonderer Atmosphäre," from *Neue Gesundheit*. Reprinted by permission of **Gräfliche Kurverwaltung, Bad Driburg, Germany.**

Holt German 2 Komm mit!, Chapter 6

Realia 6-1: *MultiVitamin* ad

1. **Reading** Have students make a list of the cognates and guess what the product is, based on the cognates they listed.

2. **Reading** Prepare a list of questions or tasks based on the ad and have students scan the text for the answers. For example: Name three vitamins found in this product. Name three minerals found in this product. What is the name of the product? What company makes this product? What word describes the way this product tastes? What is a **Brausetablette**?

3. **Speaking/Pair Work** Have students role-play a pharmacist and one of his or her customers. The customer hasn't been feeling well—he or she is tired, and has no energy—and the pharmacist recommends this product and explains why it is good. Then have them switch roles.

4. **Writing** Have students imagine that they have a friend in a German-speaking country who is not feeling well. They lived in Germany before and know this product. Have them write to their friend and tell him or her all about the product and explain why the friend should use it.

Realia 6-2: Ad for suntan products

1. **Reading** 1. Have students scan the text for cognates and make a list of those that help determine the type of product being advertised. 2. Have students match the items in this product line with the type of product each of them is:
   Sonnenschutz Gel: suntan gel   **After Sun Feuchtigkeitslotion**: moisture cream
   Sun Blocker: sun block   **Sun 8 Lippenschutz und Pflegestift**: lip balm/chapstick
   3. Have students scan the text for the following information: the name of the product; by whom it is recommended; where it can be obtained; what this product line enables one to do **"ab sofort."**

2. **Listening** Make statements about these products and have students say whether your statements are true or false. For example, **Dieses Product hat sehr viel Vitamin C. (falsch: Vitamin E)**

3. **Group Work** Have students take the information from the magazine ad and turn it into a TV commercial, which they later perform for the rest of the class.

Realia 6-3: Ad for the Kur in Bad Driburg

1. **Reading** 1. Have students look at the illustrations and the title and try to figure out what kinds of things are being advertised. (What kind of **"besondere Atmosphäre"** is being described?) 2. Have students scan for specific information, such as location, duration of the program, cost, and what activities are offered that help one achieve **"Ruhe und Abwechslung"** while participating in the program.

2. **Reading** Have students match some of the words used in the text with English definitions:
   Krankengymnastik *orthopedic exercises*   **Elektrotherapie** *electro-stimulation therapy*
   Rückenschule *back therapy*   **Autogenes Training** *autogenous training (self-hypnosis)*

3. **Writing** Have students imagine that they are going to Bad Driburg. Have them write to their German pen pal, who may come to visit them while they are taking this **Kur**. They should describe the program and what the two of them can do when the pen pal comes to visit.

Immobilien	Mittwoch/Donnerstag den 13./14. Dezember 2000

Nicht genug Platz für so was?
Schauen wir mal!

Nicht alltägliches Haus im Bad Soden-Salmünster

Großes Einfamilienhaus in herrlicher ruhiger Südwestlage mit Fernblick, Bj. 1930, 6 Zimmer, Küche, Bad und Hobbyraum, Grundstücksgröße 450 m^2, sofort beziehbar.
Kaufpreis € **183 000,–**
Besichtigen Sie noch heute!

Ausschreibung 2000 Neubau-Erstbezug Große 4 Zimmer-Eigentumswohnung in Wächtersbach

Diese gut geschnittene 4 Zimmer-Wohnung mit 98 m^2 Wohnfläche wird Sie begeistern. Ein 35 m^2 großer Wohn-/Eßbereich, 3 Schlafzimmer, Südbalkon, eigene Gastherme und Fahrstuhl sind Ausstattungsmerkmale, die Sie für € **174 000,–** fast nicht mehr erhalten. Zu besichtigen!

Für Schnellentschlossene in Büdingen-Eckhartshausen

Nur sage und schreibe € **159 000,–** kostet dieses kleine, 1970 erbaute Wohnhaus mit 3 Zimmern, Küche, Bad, Balkon und 250 m^2 Grundstück. Sofortbezug. Kommen Sie zur Besichtigung!

Neubau-Doppelhaushälfte in Linsengericht-Eidengesäß

mit 529 m^2 Grundstück je Haushälfte in anspruchsvoller Wohnlage. Die schicke Architektur im Landhausstil mit versetzten Wohnebenen bietet großzügige Raumaufteilung auf 118 m^2 Wohnfläche, die Sie begeistern wird. Bezug Ende Februar.
Kaufpreis € **269 000,–**
Wir informieren Sie gerne!

Schlüchtern-Elm

3 zusammenliegende Baugrundstücke in sehr ruhiger Ortsrandlage mit angrenzender freier Natur, nicht erschlossen, ab 720 m^2.
Preis: ab **65 700,–** €

Mittel-Gründau

Ein Traumhaus für 1-2 Familien in idyllischer, ruhiger Ortsrandlage, m. off. Kamin, EBK, u.v. m. EG: 112 m^2 Wfl., DG: 74 m^2 Wfl., 1.000 m^2 Grdst. Erfüllen Sie sich diesen Traum!
Preis **340 000,–** €

Name _____ Klasse _____ Datum _____

**STEIGAUF.
SCHAUKELN!
AAH!**

Zu Hause verdienen Sie
Erleichterung. So wie mit
STEIGAUF, dem entspan-
nenden Schaukelerlebnis.
Steigauf kommt Ihnen
immer entgegen, Sie kön-
nen sogar die Kopfstütze
verstellen. Aufsteigen und
wohlfühlen, so oft Sie
wollen. Wählen Sie vorher
Muster, Stoffe und die
Telefonnummer.
Lust auf das entspan-
nende Schaukelerlebnis?
Wir informieren Sie
kostenlos! Wählen Sie
02209 / 88414
oder schreiben Sie an:
Proanima,
Hyacinthenstraße 59,
51491 Overath

Realia 7-3

Beton-Bauteile für den Gartenbau

Tips und Tricks zum Selbermachen

Der Garten ist für lärm- und streß-geplagte Stadtbewohner ein Refugium der Ruhe und Entspannung, besonders aber in Städten auch ökologisch wichtig.

Unsere kostenlose Broschüre zeigt Ihnen in zahlreichen Bildern, wie Sie Ihren Garten mit den dauerhaf-ten Beton-Bauteilen ansprechend gestalten können.

Fordern Sie diese Broschüre an bei:

Beton-Bauteile Baumann
Postfach 21 02 67, 53158 Berlin
Tel: 01 23/96 45 6-9
Fax: 01 28/95 44 6-89

Realia 7-1: Classified ads (houses, condominiums)

1. **Reading** 1. Have students first figure out what kinds of texts these are (classified ads) and what is being advertised (houses and condos). Have them find words and phrases that give them information about what kind of apartments and houses these are (price, size, words such as **groß, gut geschnitten, schicke Architektur**). 2. Have students match each ad with English summaries or descriptive phrases. For example, which ad is for a large one-family house with a hobby room? a condominium with a balcony and its own elevator?

2. **Listening** Make statements about the houses and apartments in the ads and have students say whether your statements are true or false. For example, **Das Haus in Büdingen-Eckhartshausen ist teurer als die Eigentumswohnung in Wächtersbach.** (false—The condominium is more expensive.)

3. **Writing/Pair Work** Have pairs of students write a brief letter to this real estate company describing the house or apartment that they are looking for. You might want to give each pair specific parameters: one pair is a young professional couple, one pair the parents of a large family, two of them are students looking for something inexpensive, and another pair represents a couple who have just inherited a large sum of money and are looking for their dream house.

4. **Speaking/Pair Work** After students have completed the writing activity above, have them role-play an exchange between a customer who has written the letter and the real estate agent. Have them discuss the customer's needs and then look at these six ads to figure out if one of these houses or condos meets their wishes. Have students perform their scenario for the rest of the class.

Realia 7-2: Rocking chair ad

1. **Listening** Make statements about the ad and have students say whether your statements are true or false. For example, **Der Katalog für diese Möbel kostet nichts. (stimmt)**

2. **Speaking/Pair Work** Have two students working together play the roles of a telemarketer and the person who receives the telephone call. The telemarketer is trying to sell the rocking chair in this ad, so he or she tells the potential customer all about it—mentioning what the chair offers, how to order it, etc. The other person reacts and asks questions.

3. **Writing** Have students create their own chair (or another piece of furniture) and write an ad for it. Give them the choice of writing a magazine ad or a TV commercial.

Realia 7-3: Ad for landscaping the garden

1. **Reading** Have students scan the text and tell you what it is about. What is the ad actually for? (a brochure that tells how you can use concrete fixtures to make your garden more attractive) Is this an ad for people who live in the city or for people who live in the country?

2. **Writing** Have students imagine that they live in a large city in Germany and that they are trying to make an attractive garden on the roof of their apartment house. They should write a brief letter to this company, in which they describe their living situation and briefly explain what they want their garden to look like and to do for them.

3. **Speaking/Pair Work** Using the letters they wrote in #2 above, have pairs of students play the roles of customer and salesperson. Have students carry on an imaginary telephone conversation between these two people.

4. **Writing/Group Work** Have small groups of students use this ad as a starting point to create a brochure that contains different examples of the concrete structures mentioned in this ad. The brochure should have some illustrations and information about price, size, etc. of the structures.

Realia 8-1

Bestell Mode!

Hellblaue Bluse:
24,90 €
In A-Linie, mit stoffbezogenen Knöpfen. Aus reiner Baumwolle,
Größe S-XL;
Bestell-Nr. G 13 628

Knallgelbes Hemd:
29,90 €
Weit geschnitten mit Kragen, Knopfleiste und aufgesetzter Brusttasche. Aus reinem Leinen,
Größe S-XL;
Bestell-Nr. 15 620

Kleid:
84 €
Aus kirschroter Seide Schmal geschnitten. Raffinierte Details: ein überlanger Schalkragen.
Größe 34-42;
Bestell-Nr. Y 13 623

Weite Hose:
39 €
Mit schwarzweißem Muster und Gummizug im Rücken. Aus Viskose,
Größe 36, 38/40, 42;
Bestell-Nr. N 24 639

Weste:
34,90 €
Im neuen Look! Schmalgeschnitten + mit Gürtel, aus 55% Polyacryl und 45% Baumwolle in Braun.
Größe 34-42;
Bestell-Nr. 344 209

REALIA

Realia 8-3

Realia 8-1: Ad for sportswear

1. **Reading** Have students scan the ad for adjectives that describe the kinds of clothing advertised and the types of people who wear this sports clothing. What words are used to make this type of sportswear appealing? Who would find this type of clothing attractive? (young, dynamic, active; unique, exclusive; people who like to think that they are "cut from a different mold")

2. **Reading/Writing** Using the icons as a guide, have students make a list of different sports in which one could participate wearing *Conrad Schmidt Sportswear*.

3. **Speaking/Pair Work** Have students role-play a telephone conversation between a person who wants more information about this sportswear and would like to order certain things, and a person who works in customer service at *Conrad Schmidt Sportswear*.

Realia 8-2: Clothing ads

1. **Listening** Make statements about the clothing items on this catalogue page and have students say whether your statements are true or false. For example, **Die Hose mit schwarzweißem Muster ist billiger als die hellblaue Bluse.**

2. **Speaking/Writing/Pair Work** Have pairs of students use this catalogue page to create an outfit that will be modeled in an upcoming fashion show. Have them write a description of the outfit that can be read at the fashion show.

3. **Pair Work** Have pairs of students play the roles of a customer ordering some of these clothes by phone and the salesperson who takes down the order. The person who takes the order should read it back to confirm accuracy.

Realia 8-3: Jeans ad

1. **Listening** Make statements about the ad and have students say whether your statements are true or false.

2. **Speaking** Ask questions about the ad, such as **Was sind die neuen Farben für die neuen Jeans? Wie viele verschiedene Jeans-Modelle gibt es in diesem Geschäft?**

3. **Speaking** Have students study the illustrations at the bottom of the ad and tell you in German what "story" they represent. (The stick-figure gets on his or her bicycle, goes to *Magazzino*, finds a pair of jeans, buys the jeans, pays for them, and rides back home—happy!)

4. **Speaking/Pair Work** Have pairs of students play the roles of two students in Germany. One of them lives in Berlin and has just discovered *Magazzino*, and the other lives in another city and is coming to Berlin for a visit. The **Berliner(in)** tells the other all about the new jeans store, and they make plans to go there during the visit.

5. **Writing** Have students write a note (such as they might write to another student in class) telling another person all about the new *Magazzino* in Berlin. They should mention what types of jeans are available there, when the store is open, and where it is located.

Realia 9-1

SPORT IN DER GRUPPE

Reisen Sie mit uns!

Haben Sie Lust auf Sport im Urlaub?

Aerobic • Bergwandern • Ballonfahren
Bogenschießen • Bungee-Jumping • Kanadier
Darts • Drachenfliegen • Eisfallklettern
Fallschirmspringen • Freeclimbing
Gleitschirmfliegen • Golf • Gletschertouren
Heliski • Inselwandern • Iglubauen • Kajak
Kanu • Klettern • Langlauf • Motorboot
Mountainbike • Paddeln • Radfahren • Reiten
Radwandern • Rafting • Schneeschuhtrekking
Schnorcheln • Schwimmen • Segelfliegen
Segeltörns • Skifahren • Snowboarding • Surfen
Snowrafting • Tauchen • Tennis • Telemark
Tourenski • Trekking • Tanzen • Volleyball
Wandern • Wasserski • Wellenreiten
Wildwasserfahrten • Yoga ...

Lassen Sie sich von uns beraten!

**REISEBÜRO MEIER
KARLSRUHE
TELEFON (0721) 471 13 09**

REALIA

Kofferpacken für die Ferien

Das sollten Sie rechtzeitig vor dem Kofferpacken erledigen:

☐ Autoinspektion

☐ Impfen (für bestimmte Reiseländer)

☐ Arzt

☐ Zahnarzt

☐ Apotheke

☐ Drogerie

☐ Reinigung

☐ Schuster

☐ Friseur

Das gehört zum Reisegepäck:

☐ Ausweis- und Grenz-papiere

☐ ausländisches Bargeld

☐ eurocheques und eurocheque-Karte

☐ Reiseschecks

☐ evtl. Benzingutscheine

☐ Flugtickets, Hotelgut-scheine oder ähnliche, schon vorbereitete Reisepapiere

☐ Reiselektüre

☐ Weitere Informationen über das Urlaubsland

☐ Fotoapparat

☐ Filmkamera

☐ Filme

☐ Sonnenbrille

☐ Sonnenöl

☐ Schmerztabletten

☐ Pflaster, Verband

☐ sonstige Medikamente

☐ Spielsachen

☐ Hausschlüssel

☐ Badesachen

_____

☐ Kleider _____

_____

_____

_____

_____

_____

_____

☐ Schuhe _____

_____

☐ Sonstiges _____

_____

_____

_____

_____

_____

REALIA

Realia 9-3

Terramar:

Urlaub, der berauscht.

Das Hotel Le Touessrok auf Mauritius: Im Rausch der Sinne. Angefangen bei den Sport- möglichkeiten bis hin zur Einsamkeit des Muschelsuchers. Mehr aufregende Urlaubstips im Fernreisekatalog, den Sie auch gebührenfrei bestel- len können. Hörmuschel abheben, 0130/4480 wählen, und schon rauscht er ins Haus.

DIE KLEINE REISEGESELLSCHAFT

Excerpt from advertisement, "Terramar: Urlaub, der berauscht.," from *Focus*. Reprinted by permission of **Michael Conrad & Leo Burnett GmbH & Co. KG**.

Realia 9-1: "Sports on vacation" ad

1. **Speaking/Pair Work** Have students work with a partner and go through the list of sports to make sure they understand what they are. Then have them discuss together which sports appeal to them and make a list of those sports for each person.

2. **Speaking/Pair Work** Have pairs of students come up with some potential vacation spots where these sports and activities might take place. For example, **Iglubauen** could be in Alaska, while **Inselwandern** might be in Majorca or Hawaii.

3. **Pair Work** Have students switch partners. One person in the new pair is a customer, and the other is a travel agent. The customer is interested in a vacation during which he or she can participate in a lot of sports. The travel agent mentions several places where this might be possible and tells the customer what sports and activities would be available in each place. Students should then switch roles.

Realia 9-2: Travel checklist

1. **Reading** Go through the checklist with students and make sure they understand all the items on the list. Ask them for what kind of trip they might need such a checklist. Have students list all the places they would need to go in order to complete the checklist. When they have figured out all the places, have them categorize the items on the checklist according to the places they listed. For example, **ausländisches Bargeld** would be listed under **Bank**.

2. **Group Work** Have students in small groups imagine that they are a family preparing for a trip. The tasks for getting ready for the trip should be divided among the members of the "family." Have them discuss first who is to take care of each task, and then, just before the trip, have them find out if everyone did everything he or she was supposed to do.

Realia 9-3: Ad for a travel magazine

1. **Reading** Have students look for cognates and/or any words or expressions that will help them figure out what this ad is for. Once they have figured out the word **Urlaubstips,** have them read the text to determine what kinds of tips are offered. Can they also figure out how the word **Hörmuschel** is used in this text? Why is that word used here?

2. **Writing/Pair Work** Have pairs of students create their own travel magazine.

Name _____ Klasse _____ Datum _____

Realia 10-1

INTELLIVISION CTV-4321 II
51-cm Farbfernseher (sichtbar 49,5), Kabeltuner, 32
Programme, automatischer Sendersuchlauf, AV-
Direkteingang, Kopfhöreranschluß, **Fernbedienung.**

1.5. **Zeitkaufrate*** 3.–
**Finanzierungs-
preis** 237.97

224.–

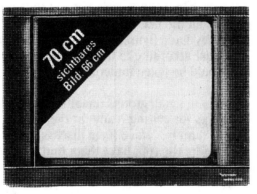

HOFFMANN STV-7676
70-cm-Stereo-Farbfernseher (sichtbar 66 cm),
Videotext mit 8 Seitenspeicher, Kabeltuner, 50 Watt,
Hyperband/Kabeltuner, 30 Programmspeicher,
Fernbedienung.

1.5. **Zeitkaufrate*** 9.–
**Finanzierungs-
preis** 635.47

599.–

REALIA

Sie brauchen für alle Geräte jetzt nur noch eine Fernbedienung: die Toptel 1.

Für immer mehr Geräte im Haushalt gibt es Fernbedienungen: Für Fernsehgeräte, Videorecorder, CD-Player, Tuner, Stereoanlagen, Satellitenempfänger usw. Und manchmal geht das Suchen nach der richtigen Fernbedienung ganz schön auf die Nerven... Doch jetzt hat das Suchen ein Ende – diese sensationelle Fernbedienung ist eine für alle und alles! Durchdachte Tastenanordnung, einfachste Bedienung, modernes Styling und die neue Technologie machen dieses High-Tech-Produkt zukunftssicher und begehrt, in den Maßen 170 x 60 mm. Diese IR-Fernbedienung können Sie ganz schnell erhalten: für nur einen neuen FUNK Uhr-Abonnenten.

CME

REALIA

"Sie brauchen für alle Geräte jetzt nur noch eine Fernbedienung: die Toptel 1." from *FUNK UHR*. Reprinted by permission of **Axel Springer Verlag**.

Realia 10-3

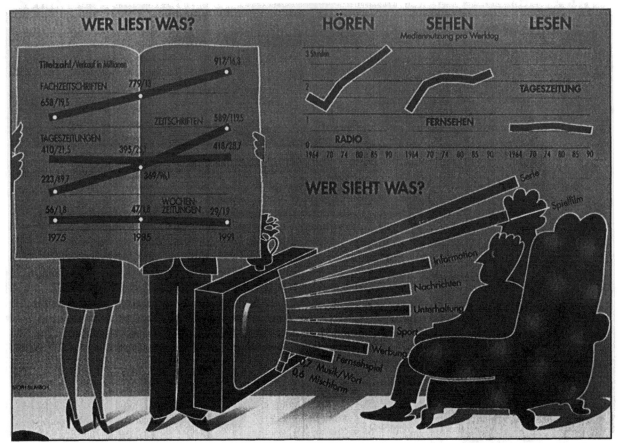

"Wer liest was?...Wer sieht was?" from *Deutschland*. Reprinted by permission of *Frankfurter Societäts-Druckerei GmbH.*

Realia 10-1: Ads for television sets

1. **Reading** Have students work with the text to find out such details as cost, size of screen, and capabilities of the TVs. Have them convert the figures and compare the price with a similar TV in the United States. Are these TVs considered "large screen" TVs? How does the price compare to a similar TV in this country? See if students can figure out why there are two prices given for each TV. (cash vs. credit)

2. **Listening** Make statements about the two ads and have students say whether your statements are true or false. For example, **Der 51-cm-Farbfernseher hat Kopfhöreranschluss, aber leider keine Fernbedienung.** (false—Der 51-cm-Farbfernseher hat beides.)

3. **Speaking/Pair Work** Have pairs of students play the roles of customer and salesperson. The customer is looking for a new TV and is interested in the two TVs pictured here. He or she is leaning toward the less expensive set but the salesperson is trying to convince him or her that the **70-cm-Fernseher** would be a better buy.

Realia 10-2: Remote control ad

1. **Reading** Have students identify all the cognates that help them figure out the text. Have them tell you which electrical appliances mentioned can be controlled with a remote control. Make sure they understand which features make this remote control "**zukunftssicher und begehrt.**" (well-thought-out order of buttons on control; uncomplicated to use; modern styling; latest technology) Explain to them that this remote control can be obtained by subscribing to the magazine *FUNK-Uhr*.

2. **Speaking/Pair Work** Have students imagine that their family just acquired this remote control. The student calls a friend and explains all about the remote control and how it functions. The friend is not very high-tech and asks a lot of questions.

Realia 10-3: Survey about reading vs. television vs. radio

1. **Listening** Make statements about the survey results and have students say whether your statements are true or false. If they are false, students should correct them. For example, **Die meisten Leute, die fernsehen, sehen sich Sportsendungen an.** (false; most of them watch series, such as sitcoms)

2. **Writing/Speaking** Have each student write five questions about these survey results and five proposed answers to the questions. Then have them ask the class their questions and confirm the accuracy of their answers.

Realia 11-1

Theatervorschau vom 26.8-15.9.

	Berliner Ensemble 1040, Am Bertolt-Brecht-Platz, Tel: 282 31 60, Friedrichstr.	Berliner Kammer-spiele 21. Alt-Moabit 99 Tel: 391 55 43 U-Bhf. Turmstr., Bus 101, 123, 245, VVK: Mo-Sa 10-19, So+Feier-tag 15-18 h	Deutsche Oper Berlin 12. Bismarckstr. 35 Tel: 341 02 49, U-Dt. Oper, Bus 101, Wk: Mo-Sa 11.30-17.30, So 10-14 u. 1 Std. vor Beginn	Deutsche Staats-oper 1080 Unter den Linden 7, Tel. 200 47 62, U- Friedrichstr., S- Marx-Engels Platz	Deutsches Theater 1040, Schumann-str. 13a Tel: 264 41-0, Mo-Sa 12-18.30 VVK 28441225 U/S-Bhf. Friedrich-straße, Bus 147
Mittwoch **1.** Sept	Programm bitte telefonisch erfragen		17.30 Der Ring des Nibelungen	20.00 Festwochen-konzert	20.00 Iphigenia (Garten)
Donnerstag **2.**	Programm bitte telefonisch erfragen	19.00 Andorra	19.30 Aida	20.00 I Capuleti e i Montecchi	20.00 Iphigenia (Garten)
Freitag **3.**	Programm bitte telefonisch erfragen	19.00 Andorra	19.30 Dornröschen (Ballett)	19.30 Hoffmanns Erzählungen	20.00 Iphigenia (Garten)
Samstag **4.**	Programm bitte telefonisch erfragen	19.00 Andorra	19.30 Die Zarenglocken von St. Petersburg	19.30 Nacht/Verklärte Nacht/Der wunder-bare Mandarin	19.30 Der Diener zweier Herren
Sonntag **5.**	Programm bitte telefonisch erfragen		17.00 Der Ring des Nibelungen	19.00 Nacht/Verklärte Nacht/Der wunder-bare Mandarin	19.30 Reineke Fuchs

Excerpts from "tip-programm" from *tip BerlinMagazin.* Copyright © by TIP-Magazin, Verlag Klaus Stemmler. Reprinted by permission of *TIP-Magazine, Verlag Klaus Stemmler.*

SCHÖNER

ESSEN &

TRINKEN

IN BERLIN

2 Minuten vom Ku'damm

Das erste indische
SPEZIALITÄTENRESTAURANT
in Berlin seit über 25 Jahren

BOMBAY
RESTAURANT

große vegetarische Auswahl
täglich geöffnet von 12 - 24 Uhr

exclusiv: mit orig. ind. Tandouri

Bleibtreustraße 12 - 2000 Berlin 11
Telefon 881 61 90

MAN TRIFFT SICH IM
Quincy

GRUNEWALDSTRASSE 11
1000 Berlin 22
zwischen Ⓤ Eisenacher + Kleistpark
Tel. 211 55 33

geöffnet
18.00 – ?

鹽鹽鹽鹽鹽鹽鹽!
*Berlins
älteste
griechische
Taverna*

PANTHEON

Wielandstraße 33 1000 Berlin 11
Telefon: 333 77 43
Öffnungszeiten: 12.00-02.00 Uhr
– täglich wechselnde Tageskarte –
鹽鹽鹽鹽鹽鹽鹽鹽鹽鹽鹽!

La Distancia

Typisch Lateinamerikanische
Spezialitäten

geöffnet 18.30 – 2.00 Uhr
Küche bis 1.00 Uhr

Bundesallee 21, Berlin
Telefon 761 21 11
U-Bahn Berliner Str., Bus 104 + 204

REALIA

Realia 11-3

HOTEL-RESTAURANT
HAUS *Dannenberg* AM SEE
Speisenkarte

VORSPEISEN
Gefülltes Ei auf Gemüsesalat	2,70
Geräuchertes Forellenfilet	3,25

SUPPEN
Nudelsuppe mit Huhn	2,10
Frische Gemüsesuppe	2,00

BEILAGEN
Portion Sauerkraut	1,90
Portion Pommes frites	1,75
Portion Gemüse	2,10
Salatteller	2,25
Kloß	1,50
Scheibe Brot	0,35

HAUPTGERICHTE

FISCHGERICHTE
Mit Lachs gefüllte Seezungenröllchen mit Brokkoli-Rahmsauce	12,50
Filets vom Babysteinbutt mit Walnußsauce auf einem Gemüsebett serviert	11,25
Gegrilltes Seebarschfilet m. Salzkartoffeln und gemischtem Gemüse	12,30
Frische Seezunge nach Art des Hauses m. Salzkartoffeln u. gem. Salat	13,25

FLEISCHGERICHTE
Wiener Schnitzel m. Salzkartoffeln oder Pommes frites	11,25
Königsberger Klopse m. Nudeln und gemischtem Salat	8,40
Ungarisches Gulasch mit Kloß	5,95
Frische mecklenburgische Mastente mit Kartoffelkloß	9,25
Schweinerückensteak mit Kräuterbutter u. Pommes frites	10,65

NACHSPEISEN
Rote Grütze mit Vanillesauce	2,30
Apfelstrudel	1,90
Frische Erdbeeren mit Sahne	3,45

GETRÄNKE

WARME GETRÄNKE
1 Tasse Kaffee	1,90
1 Kännchen Kaffee	3,00
1 Tasse Tee	1,90
1 Tasse Kaffee Hag	2,15

ALKOHOLFREIE GETRÄNKE
Mineralwasser	0,3/	1,90
Apfelsaft	0,4/	1,80
Orangensaft	0,3/	1,50
Fruchtlimo	0,3/	1,50

ALKOHOLISCHE GETRÄNKE
Verlangen Sie bitte unsere Getränkekarte

REALIA

Realia 11-1: Calendar of cultural events

1. **Reading** Have students study the schedule and answer questions about it. How is it set up? How many different areas are covered by the schedule? (classical music/concerts, opera, theater) Which of the five groups represented in the schedule does not have something offered every day? Which schedule has to be learned by phone? What cultural events are available on Saturday, September 4?

2. **Listening** Make statements about when you want to do certain things and have students tell you what event you are talking about. For example, **Ich gehe am Sonntag, den 5. September um 19.30 ins Theater. (Du siehst eine Aufführung von Reineke Fuchs.)** Or make statements about what you are going to see and have students tell you when and where you will see it: **Ich sehe eine Aufführung von *Iphigenia*. (Du gehst am Donnerstag um 20.00 ins Deutsche Theater.)**

3. **Writing** Have students imagine that they are exchange students in Berlin. Their German pen pal is coming for a visit and is very interested in cultural activities such as concerts, theater, and opera. Have them write a letter to the pen pal telling him or her what will be available on certain days. The student should tell the pen pal what his or her preferred activities are, so that they can discuss it together and make a plan for the upcoming visit.

4. **Speaking/Pair Work** Have pairs of students pretend to be the exchange student living in Berlin and the visiting pen pal from the activity above. Have them carry on a telephone conversation in which they discuss the possible activities, their personal preferences, and a plan that will be satisfactory to both of them.

Realia 11-2: Ads for specialty restaurants

1. **Reading** First have students determine what kind of ads these are (ads for specialty restaurants). Then have them figure out what kinds of cuisine are represented in the ads. (Indian, Greek, Latin American)

2. **Reading/Writing/Pair Work** Have students write two questions about each ad. Have them work with a partner to ask and answer the questions that each of them has written.

3. **Group Work** Have small groups of students imagine that they are visiting Berlin and are trying to decide which restaurant to go to on a specific evening. They should discuss the pros and cons of each restaurant and make a decision about where they are going to go.

Realia 11-3: Menu

1. **Reading** Give students a list of different clients in the restaurant and have them put together a possible menu for each of those persons. For example, an older couple with a lot of money; a student; a woman who likes fish but doesn't like potatoes; etc.

2. **Speaking/Pair Work** Have pairs of students role-play problem situations that could take place in a restaurant such as the **Haus Dannenberg am See**. Some examples: a very rich and somewhat snobbish gentleman ordered the **Gemüsesuppe** but was brought the **Nudelsuppe mit Huhn**—he hates noodles; a woman who is allergic to bell peppers ordered the **Königsberger Klopse** but was brought the **ungarisches Gulasch mit Kloß**; several people in a group—all of whom are very hungry—ordered dinners, but the waiter got their orders mixed up with the people at the next table; the waiter made a mistake in tallying up one person's bill.

Name _____ Klasse _____ Datum _____

Realia 12-1

Advertisement, "Party...hfc.," from *tip BerlinMagazin*.
Reprinted by permission of *hfc.: Helmuts Fahrrad-Center*.

REALIA

Restaurants - international
– Anzeigen –

Italienisch

Al Canale Ristorante
Pizza, Pasta und italienische Spezialitäten vom Feinsten, tägl. 12-15, 18-24 Uhr, Montag Ruhetag Königstr. 1, Elmshorn, Tel. 04121/1221

Ristorante Pein
Gute, italienische Küche, frischer Lachs, Gambas, Scampi aus der Riesenpfanne, Gute Musik, auch live. Geöffnet v. Di.-So. 12-15 u. 18-24 Uhr. Sa. ab 10 Uhr. Carl-Zeiss-Str. 8, 2085 Quickborn, Tel. 04106/72611

La Compagnia
Pizza aller Variationen, ausgefallene Pasta-Gerichte neue u. bekannte Spez. aus den Provinzen, tägl. frische Muscheln. Mo.-Fr. 12-15 u. 17.30-24.00 Uhr. Sa., Son. 12-24 Uhr. Altonaer Chaussee 22-30, 2000 Schenefeld, Tel. 040/8301122

Ristorante Sorrento
Italienischer Charme in Hemdingen. Vielfältige Speisen, ausgesuchte Weine. Räumlichkeiten f. Gesellschaften aller Art, Steindamm 1, 2081 Hemdingen, Tel. 04123/7887

Chinesisch

China Restaurant Canton
Sämtl. Gerichte auch außer Haus tägl. v. 11.30-15.00 und 17.30-23.00 Uhr, Mittagstisch, Meßtorffstr. 47, 2082 Uetersen, Tel.:04122/47793

Thailändisch

Win On
Das erste thailändische Restaurant im Kreis Pinneberg Geöffnet von So.-Fr. 11.30-14.30 und 18.30-23.30 Uhr. Sa. nur 18.30-23.30 Uhr. Markstr. 29, Uetersen, Tel. 04122/44365

Griechisch

Restaurant Caesar
der etwas andere Grieche... Speisen auf ungewohnte Art. Rosenstr. 17, 2206 Sparrieshop Tel: 04121/85719

Taverna Michali
Griechische Spezialitäten Restaurant. Geöffnet tägl. 17.30-24.00 Uhr, warme Küche bis 23.30 Uhr. Sonn. u. feiertags auch 11.30-15.00 Uhr. Fröbelstr. 13, Pinneberg, Tel. 04101/63128

Ristorante „Al Canale"
Pizza & Pasta · ital. Spezialitäten täglich außer Mont. 12-15 + 18-24 Uhr Elmshorn, Königstr. 1, Tel. 0 41 21-12 21

China - Restaurant
CANTON
Ngoc Hung Tien
25436 Uetersen · Meßtorffstraße 47 · Telefon (0 41 22) 4 77 93

45

"Restaurants-international" from *Kreis Pinneberg Führer.* Reprinted by permission of **RASTA-Verlag.**

Realia 12-3

Advertisement, "Buttermilch!," from *stern magazin*. Reprinted by permission of **Centrale Marketing Gesellschaft der deutschen Agrarwirtschaft mbH.**

Realia 12-1: Ad for a bicycle shop

1. **Reading** Have students scan the text for words that help make it clear what the text is about. Make sure they understand that the text is about a bicycle shop, not just the bicycles. Have them find the words and phrases that refer to the place and those that describe the new bicycles. What event is going to take place on August 14?

2. **Speaking** Ask students questions about the text to make sure they have understood the content. For example, **Was ist HFC? Wenn man ein Fahrrad kauft, wie lange muss man warten, bis man das Fahrrad bekommt?**

3. **Speaking/Pair Work** Have pairs of students role-play a new employee at the new HFC and a friend of his or hers. The employee is very excited about the new place and is telling the friend all about it. Students should then switch roles.

4. **Writing** Have students imagine that they are the new manager of the HFC and that they want to invite a number of important people to the opening of the new shop. Have them write an invitation that could be sent to such people as the mayor, a councilman, etc. The invitation should say something about the new place as well as give details about the opening, such as date and time.

Realia 12-2: Restaurant ads

1. **Listening** Make statements about the restaurants in the ads and have students say whether the statements are true or false.

2. **Writing/Pair Work** Have students write two questions about each ad. Then have them get together with a partner and answer each other's questions.

3. **Speaking/Group Work** Have students imagine that they are with a group of students in Berlin. They want to eat out, but they are having a hard time making a decision about where to go. Have the ads here represent their different choices. Each one should tell the others in the group where he or she wants to go, what he or she can eat there, when the restaurant is open, etc.

Realia 12-3: Ad for buttermilk

1. **Reading** Make sure students understand the text. What connection do they think there might be between the mention of this woman's clothes and what she is drinking?

2. **Speaking** Have the students describe the woman, both the way she looks and what kind of person they think she is.

3. **Writing** Have students think of different captions that can go into the speech bubble. Have them write those captions in the bubble and read them to each other.

4. **Writing/Group Work** Have students in small groups convert this magazine ad into a TV commercial. Have each group perform its commercial for the rest of the class; if possible, videotape the presentations.

Situation Cards

Situation Cards 1-1, 1-2, 1-3: Interview

Situation 1-1: Interview

I have been sent by the school newspaper to collect opinions about the teachers in your school. Tell me what you think about certain teachers in your school by answering these questions.

Welche Lehrer findest du nett? Welche nicht?

Wen findest du sympathisch/unsympathisch? Warum?

Wer ist immer/manchmal/selten/oft gut oder schlecht gelaunt?

Von wem lernst du am meisten? In welchem Fach?

Situation 1-2: Interview

How would you describe students in your class? Answer these questions:

Wer trägt heute Ohrringe, eine Halskette oder ein Armband?

Wie sehen die Ohrringe aus?/ Wie sieht die Halskette oder das Armband aus?

Wer trägt im Winter einen Schal oder eine Mütze? Wie sehen die aus?

Was trägt (John) heute?

Was trägst du?

Situation 1-3: Interview

I am an athletics trainer and I am looking for students to join my club. Tell me which sports you like and which you dislike.

Welche Leichtathletiksportarten magst du (zum Beispiel Kugelstoßen, Speerwerfen, Weitsprung)?

Was magst du nicht?

In welchen Sportarten bist du besonders gut? In welchen bist du nicht besonders gut? Kannst du, zum Beispiel, schnell laufen? Hoch springen?

SITUATION CARDS

Situation Cards 1-1, 1-2, 1-3: Role-playing

Situation 1-1: Role-playing

Student A   You and **Student B** exchange opinions about different teachers. Say whether you think a certain teacher is nice, friendly, unfriendly, smart, and so on. Give reasons why you like or do not like certain teachers. Ask for your partner's opinion.

Student B   You and **Student A** exchange opinions on different teachers. **Student A** will tell you what he or she thinks about a certain teacher. Agree with him or her, or tell him or her how you would describe the teacher. Your partner will also ask you to name some teachers whom you especially like or dislike.

Situation 1-2: Role-playing

Student A   Select a student in your class who is wearing something striking: earring(s), a necklace, a hat or something similar (use the vocabulary of this chapter). **Student B** will ask you questions to find out who it is. Answer **Student B**'s questions until he or she is able to figure out who it is. Example: **Trägt diese Person Ohrringe? Wie sehen die Ohrringe aus?—Ja, diese Person trägt goldene Ohrringe.**

Student B   Student A has selected someone in your class who is wearing something striking: earring(s), a necklace, a hat, or something similar. Ask **Student A** questions in order to find out who that person is. (Use the vocabulary of this chapter.) Example: **Trägt diese Person einen grünen Schal?—Nein, diese Person trägt keinen Schal.**

Situation 1-3: Role-playing

Student A   Ask **Student B** which sports he or she likes and which he or she dislikes. Then answer his or her questions.

Student B   Answer **Student A**'s questions about the sports you like and don't like to do. Then ask him or her similar questions.

SITUATION CARDS

Situation Cards 2-1, 2-2, 2-3: Interview

Situation 2-1: Interview

Imagine that I am a relative of yours, and that your mother complained to me that you do not help enough at home. You might want to argue that this is not true and tell me how you help at home. How would you answer the following questions?

Hilfst du in der Küche? Wie? Wie oft?

Was machst du im Wohnzimmer? Staub saugen? Wischen?

Räumst du dein eigenes Zimmer auf? Wie oft? Was musst du alles machen?

Hilfst du auch beim Wäschewaschen?

Situation 2-2: Interview

Imagine I am the salesperson in a grocery store, and you are the customer who wants to buy something. How would you answer the following questions?

Wir haben heute ein Sonderangebot an Zwetschgen, Pfirsichen und Spinat. Sie möchten doch sicher etwas davon?

Sie möchten also Bohnen. Wie viel Gramm oder Kilogramm sollen es denn sein?

Sonst noch etwas?

Situation 2-3: Interview

I am a friend of yours who does not know what to give members of my family for their birthdays. How would you answer the following questions?

Was hast du deiner Mutter zum letzten Geburtstag geschenkt?

Wie findest du die Idee, meiner Oma einen Tennisschläger zu schenken?

Was könnte ich denn meinem Vater zum Geburtstag schenken?

SITUATION CARDS

Situation Cards 2-1, 2-2, 2-3: Role-playing

Situation 2-1: Role-playing

Student A   You and **Student B** are discussing how you help at home. Ask **Student B** what he or she does. Then answer his or her questions.

Student B   Answer **Student A**'s questions and say how you help at home. Then ask **Student A** what he or she does to help at home.

Situation 2-2: Role-playing

Student A   You are the salesperson at an open market. Today, you have a special on plums, bananas, peaches, beans, peas, and spinach. Try to convince the customer to buy some or all of these promotional items.

Student B   You are the customer at an open market. You are mainly looking for vegetables like spinach and peas. You might also want to buy plums and peaches. **Student A** is the salesperson. Bargain with him or her about the specials.

Situation 2-3: Role-playing

Student A   Your mother's birthday is coming up soon and you have no idea what you could give her as a present. Ask **Student B,** who always has good ideas. He or she can surely help you.

Student B   Answer **Student A**'s questions. He or she needs advice on a birthday present. Make suggestions.

SITUATION CARDS

Situation Cards 3-1, 3-2, 3-3: Interview

Situation 3-1: Interview

I would like to know which towns or areas in Germany or the United States you like, and what you can do or see there. How would you answer the following questions?

Welche Stadt magst du besonders? Warum?

Bist du selbst schon einmal dort gewesen? Wann? Für wie lange?

Was kann man dort machen?

Was kann man dort Interessantes sehen?

Was machst du am liebsten, wenn du eine Stadt besuchst?

Situation 3-2: Interview

Imagine you went to Germany last summer. I would like to know where you went and what you did there. Answer the following questions:

Wo warst du letzten Sommer?

Wie bist du dahin gekommen? Wie lange warst du da?

Was gab es dort Interessantes: Fachwerkhäuser? eine Oper? Theater? Was hat dir am besten gefallen?

Was hast du dort außerdem gesehen?

Was hast du noch gemacht?

Situation 3-3: Interview

I would like to know about one trip you took recently. Answer the following questions:

Wo bist du in den letzten Ferien gewesen?

Wie hat es dir dort gefallen?

Wo hast du dort übernachtet?

Wo hast du Frühstück/zu Mittag/Abendbrot gegessen?

Wie hat das Essen geschmeckt?

Du warst als Tourist/Touristin da—war es teuer? Kannst du mir ein Beispiel geben?

SITUATION CARDS

Situation Cards 3-1, 3-2, 3-3: Role-playing

Situation 3-1: Role-playing

Student A   Ask **Student B** which towns or areas in Germany or the United States he or she likes, why he or she likes them, and what you can do or see there. Then switch roles.

Student B   **Student A** will ask you which towns or areas in Germany or the United States you like and why, and what you can do and see there. Answer his or her questions based on what you have heard about Germany so far (you need not have been there). Then switch roles.

Situation 3-2: Role-playing

Student A   **Student B** will imagine that he or she visited a town or an area in Germany last summer. Ask **Student B** where he or she has been and what he or she did in that town or area. Then switch roles.

Student B   Imagine you visited a certain town or area in Germany last summer (it can be your favorite German town or area). **Student A** will ask you where you were and what you saw and did there. Use your imagination and what you know about the town or area to answer his or her questions. Then switch roles.

Situation 3-3: Role-playing

Student A   **Student B** recently took a trip. Ask him or her questions about the trip: where he or she went, where he or she stayed, and where he or she had most meals. Find out how he or she liked it and what he or she did there. Then switch roles.

Student B   **Student A** will ask you questions about a trip you recently took. Answer his or her questions. Use time expressions (every evening, every morning, always, after lunch, etc.) whenever he or she asks you how you spent your time. Then switch roles.

SITUATION CARDS

Situation Cards 4-1, 4-2, 4-3: Interview

Situation 4-1: Interview

You are at a health fair. I am a reporter for a German paper, and I stop you to ask you a few questions.

Wie fühlen Sie sich heute?

Was kann man tun, um sich gesund zu halten?

Was tun Sie persönlich für Ihre Gesundheit?

Situation 4-2: Interview

Your school paper wants to publish a special edition on students' lifestyles. A classmate of yours who works for the paper asks you some questions.

Wie oft machst du Sport? Welche Sportarten machst du?

Wie oft isst du Obst und Gemüse?

Du isst bestimmt auch manchmal Schokolade, oder?

Situation 4-3: Interview

You are with your host family in Germany for the first time. Your host mother asks you about your eating habits. How would you answer her questions?

Haben Sie Allergien, oder dürfen Sie alles essen?

Welches Obst und Gemüse essen Sie am liebsten?

Was mögen Sie nicht so gern und warum nicht?

SITUATION CARDS

Situation Cards 4-1, 4-2, 4-3: Role-playing

Situation 4-1: Role-playing

Student A   You are a reporter for a German newspaper, and you were sent to a health fair to collect opinions about different lifestyles. Ask **Student B**, who is visiting the health fair, how he or she thinks that people can keep themselves fit. Then ask questions about how he or she keeps him- or herself fit.

Student B   You are visiting a health fair. A reporter for a German newspaper (**Student A**) stops you to ask you a few questions. Answer his or her questions.

Situation 4-2: Role-playing

Student A   The school paper you are working for plans to publish a special edition on students' lifestyles. Ask **Student B** what kind of sports he or she does and how often. Then ask how often he or she eats certain foods like vegetables, fruit, chocolate, fish, meat, and so on.

Student B   You are a classmate of **Student A**, who works for the school paper. He or she will ask you questions for a special edition of the paper that will focus on students' lifestyles. Answer his or her questions.

Situation 4-3: Role-playing

Student A   You are the host mother or father of a German family meeting with your American guest student for the first time. Ask **Student B**, the guest student, about his or her eating habits. Ask, for instance, whether there is anything he or she must not eat because of allergies. Also ask which kinds of vegetables or fruit he or she likes to eat and which not (be sure to find out why not).

Student B   You are an American student on an exchange program in Germany. You meet with the host family for the first time. Your host father or mother will ask you questions about your eating habits. Answer his or her questions.

Holt German 2 Komm mit!, Chapter 4

SITUATION CARDS

Situation Cards 5-1, 5-2, 5-3: Interview

Situation 5-1: Interview

Imagine that you work at a snack stand in the student cafeteria and that you are out of almost everything today. When I ask you about different things, express regret at not having them. Respond to these requests.

Ich hätte gern ein Käsebrot.

Ich möchte bitte eine Limonade.

Ich esse gerne Bananen. Haben Sie noch Bananen?

Ich trinke am liebsten Milch. Haben Sie Milch?

Situation 5-2: Interview

I am a nutrition expert and it is my job to prepare a nutrition profile for each student. I will ask you questions and your answers will become part of your profile.

Was isst du normalerweise (zum Frühstück)?

Was isst du am liebsten (zum Frühstück)?

Was hast du normalerweise auf deinem Sandwich?

Isst du gern (Fleisch)? Wie oft isst du (Fleisch)?

Isst du oft (Obst)? Welches (Obst) isst du am liebsten?

Situation 5-3: Interview

The supermarket where you shop is taking a survey about customer preferences. I will ask you questions about what you like and don't like. Respond to my questions.

Welches Obst magst du lieber: (Bananen) oder (Äpfel)?

Welches Obst isst du am liebsten?

Magst du Suppe? Was magst du lieber: (Hühnersuppe) oder (Nudelsuppe)?

Welche Suppe magst du am liebsten?

Was schmeckt dir besser: (Rindfleisch) oder (Schweinefleisch)?

Was für Fleisch isst du am liebsten?

Activities for Communication **131**

SITUATION CARDS

Situation Cards 5-1, 5-2, 5-3: Role-playing

Situation 5-1: Role-playing

Student A You are helping out at the stand where students buy snacks during the **Pause.** Today, you have sold almost everything, except for **Joghurt,** a couple of **Käsebrötchen,** and **Vanillemilch.** Your partner (**Student B**) will ask you what is still available. If you do not have what he or she asks for, respond appropriately.

Student B Your school has a stand where you and other students like to buy snacks during the **Pause.** Today you are running late, and they are sold out of almost everything when you arrive. Ask **Student A,** who works there, for the food items you want. Respond appropriately if these items are sold out.

Situation 5-2: Role-playing

Student A You and your friend (**Student B**) are on a picnic together. You were responsible for bringing the main course; **Student B** was responsible for bringing a side dish and something to drink. As you unpack the picnic, show your friend what you brought and ask questions about the things he or she brought.

Student B You are with your friend (**Student A**) on a picnic. Your friend was responsible for bringing the main course; you brought a side dish and the beverages. As the two of you unpack the picnic, show your friend what you brought and ask questions about the things he or she brought.

Situation 5-3: Role-playing

Student A Discuss with **Student B** what you both like to eat, what you usually eat for breakfast, and how often you eat certain meals.

Student B Discuss with **Student A** what you both like to eat, what you usually eat for breakfast, and how often you eat certain meals.

SITUATION CARDS

Situation Cards 6-1, 6-2, 6-3: Interview

Situation 6-1: Interview

You were not in school today because you have a cold, a sore throat, and a fever. I am a classmate of yours, and I am calling you to find out what is the matter. Answer my questions.

Wie geht es dir?

Was fehlt dir?

Hast du Fieber?

Hast du (Kopfschmerzen) oder (Ohrenschmerzen)?

Soll ich dir etwas aus der Apotheke oder aus der Drogerie holen?

Situation 6-2: Interview

I am your new doctor and I need to know how you are doing, as well as something about your health record. Respond to the following questions.

Guten Tag. Wie fühlst du dich?

Tut dir was weh? Was denn?

Hast du dir in deinem Leben schon mal etwas gebrochen oder verstaucht?

Hast du dich sonst irgendwie verletzt?

Wie oft putzt du dir die Zähne?

Wie oft am Tag wäschst du dir die Hände?

Situation 6-3: Interview

You have been in the sun for too long and are not feeling well. I am a friend of yours and I want to know what's wrong with you. Respond to my questions.

Wie fühlst du dich?

Hast du Fieber?

Wie lange hast du in der Sonne gelegen?

Hattest du die Sonnenmilch nicht mit?

SITUATION CARDS

Situation Cards 6-1, 6-2, 6-3: Role-playing

Situation 6-1: Role-playing

Student A   You call a classmate of yours at home (**Student B**) because he or she was not in school today and you are concerned. Ask how he or she feels and what's wrong. Also ask whether you can get something for him or her at a drug store or a pharmacy.

Student B   You were not in school today because you have a cold, a sore throat, and a fever. One of your classmates (**Student A**) calls you out of concern. Explain what is wrong with you and respond to his or her questions.

Situation 6-2: Role-playing

Student A   You are a doctor and you need to know how your patient is doing, as well as something about his or her health record. Ask questions about how he or she is feeling, about past injuries, and about general habits (washing hands, brushing teeth, etc.).

Student B   You are a patient of **Student A,** who is your new doctor. Respond to the questions your doctor asks about your present health, past injuries, and general habits.

Situation 6-3: Role-playing

Student A   Your friend (**Student B**) was in the sun too long and does not feel very well. Ask how he or she is feeling. Then give advice about what to do to avoid getting too much sun and how to get better.

Student B   You are not feeling well because you were in the sun too long. (You are tired, and your forehead is hot.) After your friend (**Student A**) has asked you what is wrong with you, ask him or her for advice on how to avoid getting too much sun and what to do to get better.

SITUATION CARDS